C000047957

IDEAS, CONCEPTS, AND REALITY

McGill-Queen's Studies in the History of Ideas
Series Editor: Philip J. Cercone

1 Problems of Cartesianism
*Edited by Thomas M. Lennon,
John M. Nicholas, and John
W. Davis*

2 The Development of the Idea
of History in Antiquity
Gerald A. Press

3 Claude Buffier and Thomas Reid:
Two Common-Sense Philosophers
Louise Marcil-Lacoste

4 Schiller, Hegel, and Marx:
State, Society, and the Aesthetic
Ideal of Ancient Greece
Philip J. Kain

5 John Case and Aristotelianism
in Renaissance England
Charles B. Schmitt

6 Beyond Liberty and Property:
The Process of Self-Recognition
in Eighteenth-Century Political
Thought
J.A.W. Gunn

7 John Toland: His Methods,
Manners, and Mind
Stephen H. Daniel

8 Coleridge and the Inspired Word
Anthony John Harding

9 The Jena System, 1804–5:
Logic and Metaphysics
G.W.F. Hegel
*Translation edited by John W. Burbidge
and George di Giovanni
Introduction and notes by
H.S. Harris*

10 Consent, Coercion, and Limit:
The Medieval Origins of
Parliamentary Democracy
Arthur P. Monahan

11 Scottish Common Sense
in Germany, 1768–1800:
A Contribution to the
History of Critical Philosophy
Manfred Kuehn

12 Paine and Cobbett:
The Transatlantic Connection
David A. Wilson

13 Descartes and the Enlightenment
Peter A. Schouls

14 Greek Scepticism: Anti-Realist
Trends in Ancient Thought
Leo Groarke

15 The Irony of Theology and the
Nature of Religious Thought
Donald Wiebe

16 Form and Transformation:
A Study in the Philosophy
of Plotinus
Frederic M. Schroeder

17 From Personal Duties
towards Personal Rights:
Late Medieval and Early
Modern Political Thought,
c. 1300–c. 1650
Arthur P. Monahan

18 The Main Philosophical
Writings and the Novel *Allwill*
Friedrich Heinrich Jacobi
*Translated and edited by
George di Giovanni*

19 Kierkegaard as Humanist:
Discovering My Self
Arnold B. Come

20 Durkheim, Morals, and
Modernity
W. Watts Miller

21 The Career of Toleration:
John Locke, Jonas Proast,
and After
Richard Vernon

22 Dialectic of Love: Platonism
in Schiller's Aesthetics
David Pugh

23 History and Memory
in Ancient Greece
Gordon Shrimpton

24 Kierkegaard as Theologian:
Recovering My Self
Arnold B. Come

25 Enlightenment and
Conservatism in Victorian
Scotland: The Career of
Sir Archibald Alison
Michael Michie

26 The Road to Egdon Heath:
The Aesthetics of the Great
in Nature
Richard Bevis

27 Jena Romanticism and Its
Appropriation of Jakob Böhme:
Theosophy – Hagiography –
Literature
Paolo Mayer

28 Enlightenment and Community:
Lessing, Abbt, Herder, and the
Quest for a German Public
Benjamin W. Redekop

29 Jacob Burckhardt and
the Crisis of Modernity
John R. Hinde

30 The Distant Relation:
Time and Identity in Spanish-
American Fiction
Eoin S. Thomson

31 Mr Simson's Knotty Case:
Divinity, Politics, and Due Process
in Early Eighteenth-Century
Scotland
Anne Skoczylas

32 Orthodoxy and Enlightenment:
George Campbell in
the Eighteenth Century
Jeffrey M. Suderman

33 Contemplation and Incarnation:
The Theology of Marie-
Dominique Chenu
Christophe F. Potworowski

34 Democratic Legitimacy:
Plural Values
and Political Power
F.M. Barnard

35 Herder on Nationality,
Humanity, and History
F.M. Barnard

36 Labeling People: French Scholars
on Society, Race, and Empire,
1815–1849
Martin S. Staum

37 The Subaltern Appeal to
Experience: Self-Identity,
Late Modernity, and the
Politics of Immediacy
Craig Ireland

38 The Invention of Journalism
Ethics: The Path to Objectivity
and Beyond
Stephen J.A. Ward

39 The Recovery of Wonder:
The New Freedom
and the Asceticism of Power
Kenneth L. Schmitz

40 Reason and Self-Enactment
in History and Politics:
Themes and Voices
of Modernity
F.M. Barnard

41 The More Moderate Side
of Joseph de Maistre:
Views on Political Liberty
and Political Economy
Cara Camcastle

42 Democratic Society
    and Human Needs
    Jeff Noonan

43 The Circle of Rights Expands:
    Modern Political Thought
    after the Reformation, 1521
    (Luther) to 1762 (Rousseau)
    Arthur P. Monahan

44 The Canadian Founding:
    John Locke and Parliament
    Janet Ajzenstat

45 Finding Freedom: Hegel's
    Philosophy and the
    Emancipation of Women
    Sara MacDonald

46 When the French Tried
    to Be British: Party, Opposition,
    and the Quest for the Civil
    Disagreement, 1814–1848
    J.A.W. Gunn

47 Under Conrad's Eyes:
    The Novel as Criticism
    Michael John DiSanto

48 Media, Memory, and
    the First World War
    David Williams

49 An Aristotelian Account
    of Induction: Creating
    Something from Nothing
    Louis Groarke

50 Social and Political Bonds:
    A Mosaic of Contrast
    and Convergence
    F.M. Barnard

51 Archives and the Event of God:
    The Impact of Michel Foucault
    on Philosophical Theology
    David Galston

52 Between the Queen and the Cabby:
    Olympe de Gouges's
    Rights of Women
    John R. Cole

53 Nature and Nurture in French
    Social Sciences, 1859–1914
    and Beyond
    Martin S. Staum

54 Public Passion:
    Rethinking the Grounds
    for Political Justice
    Rebecca Kingston

55 Rethinking the Political:
    The Sacred, Aesthetic Politics,
    and the Collège de Sociologie
    Simonetta Falasca-Zamponi

56 Materialist Ethics and Life-Value
    Jeff Noonan

57 Hegel's *Phenomenology*:
    The Dialectical Justification
    of Philosophy's First Principles
    Ardis B. Collins

58 The Social History of Ideas
    in Quebec, 1760–1896
    Yvan Lamonde
    *Translated by Phyllis Aronoff
    and Howard Scott*

59 Ideas, Concepts, and Reality
    John W. Burbidge

IDEAS, CONCEPTS, AND REALITY

John W. Burbidge

McGill-Queen's University Press
Montreal & Kingston · London · Ithaca

© McGill-Queen's University Press 2013
ISBN 978-0-7735-4127-6 (cloth)
ISBN 978-0-7735-4165-8 (paper)

Legal deposit second quarter 2013
Bibliothèque nationale du Québec

Printed in Canada on acid-free paper that is 100% ancient forest free
(100% post-consumer recycled), processed chlorine free

This book has been published with the help of a grant from the Canadian
Federation for the Humanities and Social Sciences, through the Awards
to Scholarly Publications Program, using funds provided by the Social
Sciences and Humanities Research Council of Canada.

McGill-Queen's University Press acknowledges the support of the Canada
Council for the Arts for our publishing program. We also acknowledge
the financial support of the Government of Canada through the Canada
Book Fund for our publishing activities.

Library and Archives Canada Cataloguing in Publication

Burbidge, John, 1936–
    Ideas, concepts, and reality / John W. Burbidge.

    (McGill-Queen's studies in the history of ideas, ISSN 0711-0995)
    Includes bibliographical references and index.
    ISBN 978-0-7735-4127-6 (bound). – ISBN 978-0-7735-4165-8 (pbk.)

    1. Idea (Philosophy). 2. Concepts. 3. Mind and reality. 4. Thought and
    thinking. I. Title. II. Series: McGill-Queen's studies in the history of ideas

B105.I28B87 2013   121'.4   C2012-908101-9

This book was typeset by Interscript in 10.5/13 New Baskerville.

For Jacob

Contents

Prologue 3

PART ONE FROM IDEAS TO CONCEPTS 11

1 Frege and Psychologism 13

2 From Sensations to Ideas: The Empiricists 20

3 How Ideas Emerge: Hegel 31

4 Language 39

5 From Retentive to Mechanical Memory 48

6 Thoughts and Descartes's Rules 57

7 Second Rule: Analysis and Definition 64

8 Third Rule: Synthesis and Unity 74

9 Fourth Rule: Comprehensiveness 81

10 Conceiving 90

PART TWO TENDRILS OF THOUGHT 97

11 Hegel's *Logic* 99

12 Syllogisms 107

13 *Modus ponens et al.* 113

14 Arguments from Analogy 124

15 Linguistic Variations 136

Contents

16 Ideas and Concepts   147

Epilogue   154

Acknowledgments   165

Index   167

IDEAS, CONCEPTS, AND REALITY

Prologue

WHEN WE APPROACH THE STUDY of logic for the first time, we encounter a strange paradox. The *Oxford Concise Dictionary*[1] defines logic as the "science of reasoning, proof, thinking, or inference; ... [a] chain of reasoning, correct or incorrect use of reasoning, ability in reasoning." The gerunds[2] in the definition – "reasoning" and "thinking" – suggest the study of certain activities that the intellect or mind performs. But the sophisticated discipline designated by this definition makes no mention of mental operations, nor does it nurture skills that would make thinking more effective. Rather, it defines a number of symbols, stipulates how to fit normal thoughts into those symbols, specifies particular ways of using them, and provides standards to ensure that an argument (which is now simply a pattern of such symbols) is valid.[3] It rigorously excludes any suggestion of an actual process of reasoning.

There have been a number of attempts to modify this stark contrast. Universities have developed courses with such names as "Practical Reasoning," "Argumentation," and "Informal Logic," which concentrate on inferences that do not satisfy formalists' strict criteria of validity. These train students to assess the reliability and relevance of premises, the strength of grounds, and the temptations that arise

1 17th edition, 1982.
2 Or verbal nouns.
3 The *Oxford English Reference Dictionary* (2nd ed. rev., 2003) adds a note to the above definition: "Logic involves the systematic study of the patterns of argument and in particular of those patterns of argument that are valid."

from rhetorical devices that sound like good reasons but are in fact deceptive. And scholars have undertaken much research into the details of these operations. None the less this whole subdiscipline lives in the shadow of its more rigorous counterpart – a poor second best that may be useful at times when strict validity is not possible but whose imperfections always point towards its perfect prototype. It is almost as if its contact with the messiness of actual thinking soils and besmirches it.

This discrepancy between the pure science of logical validity and the actual processes of human reasoning has many sources. Aristotle was the first to identify certain forms of good reasoning worthy of investigation irrespective of the content that thought introduces. And his schema of valid syllogisms, later augmented by the Stoic philosophers, served as the core of all logical studies until the mid-nineteenth century. But the contrast between form and content became absolute only in the writings of Gottlob Frege.

The British empiricists had tried to explain the logic of human thought by appealing to experience. They traced inferences back to associations and grounded them in sensory encounters with the world. John Stuart Mill goes so far as to say that all the calculations of mathematics are simply the result of inductive generalizations from experience.[4] Patterns have recurred so regularly in the past that people assume them to be universal and necessary. In a similar vein, Edmund Husserl, in his early *Philosophie der Arithmetik*, attempts a psychological analysis of basic logical and mathematical notions.

In his review of Husserl's work, Frege observes that both the empiricists and Husserl committed the fallacy of "psychologism." Each individual has a distinctive psychological itinerary, which is the product of his or her particular experiences, interests, and influences. One cannot base logic or mathematics on such insecure and variable foundations. So, Frege says, we need to distinguish between two kinds of mental entities: *Vorstellungen*, or ideas, and *Begriffe*, or concepts. The first are psychological and idiosyncratic; the second are objective and independent of the minds thinking them.

I use Frege's German terms for the two kinds of entities, for English translators have not been consistent when translating them.

---

4 John Stuart Mill, *A System of Logic* (London: Longmans, 1961), Book II, Chapter vi, 164ff.

Translations of Kant or the German idealists, for example, render *Vorstellung* as "conceptualization," "picture thinking," and more recently "representation." Frege's translators have adopted the term "idea" because what he is describing matches almost exactly with Locke, Berkeley, and Hume's use of that term. *Begriff* also poses problems, for the original German has become "notion" and "comprehension" as well as "concept." To provide some consistency, I use the same terms as Frege's translators[5] and limit "idea" and "concept" to what he has in mind.

Following Frege's instructions, modern logic seeks to avoid as much as possible any psychological fallacy. It looks at concepts, with their objective independence, and sets aside all ideas, with their personal associations, for thinking and reasoning are psychological operations and hence liable to subjective distortion. This is the primary reason for the discrepancy with which we started.

But Frege is not the only one to draw a sharp distinction between *Vorstellungen*, or ideas, and *Begriffe*, or concepts. Earlier in the nineteenth century, Georg Wilhelm Friedrich Hegel wrote that "philosophy does nothing but transform ideas into thoughts – although, of course, it does go on to transform the mere thought into the concept."[6] But whereas Frege introduces an exclusive opposition, Hegel suggests that one can actually move, by way of something he calls thoughts, from mere ideas to concepts. Both operations are to function within an all-inclusive realm of thinking minds.

In my innocence of Frege's strictures, I developed an interpretation of Hegel's massive and impenetrable *Science of Logic*, one of the most difficult texts in the Western philosophical tradition. In this work, abstract terms tumble out, one after another, in a sequence of paragraphs where it seems impossible to decipher where he wants us to start and how he is taking us from one step to the next. Yet Hegel claims that he is developing a philosophical system – indeed, he says, the *Logic* is the "system of pure reason."

---

5 Even though this use of "idea" does not fit easily with Plato's appeal to ideas or forms as independent of our thoughts.

6 *G.W.F. Hegel: Encyclopaedia Logic*, trans. T.F. Geraets, W.A. Suchting, and H.S. Harris (Indianapolis: Hackett, 1991), §20, Remark, 50. I have replaced their "representation" by "idea" and demoted their "Concept" to the more mundane "concept."

In an attempt to make some systematic sense of this dense and abstract prose, I found a clue in Hegel's description of his *Logic* as "thinking about thinking." The phrase suggests that what he describes is the way our thoughts develop as they think about such abstract concepts as "being," "essence," or even "conceiving." He disdains the use of illustrative examples from experience, because he is focusing simply on the meaning of the terms being thought. But the thinking of each concept none the less introduces a dynamic movement that leads on to others.

So I developed an exposition that adopted, as the interpretive thread to navigate the labyrinth of Hegel's difficult work, an analysis of the way thought functions when it starts to understand concepts. When we focus our attention on a term to establish its limits, I claimed, our mind moves and shifts to other, related thoughts. Because our thinking is plastic enough to consider its own operations, we can then reflect back on that shift, identify its starting point and its result, and highlight the process by which thought moves from one to the other. Reflection then brings that complexity together into a single focus, introducing a kind of synthesis. And because our minds are able to integrate that synthesis into a new, unified thought, we can collapse the complex interplay into another, more detailed concept, whose meaning or sense is a function of the processes through which thought has moved in reaching it. Since none of this required any imaginative correlate, I provided few if any illustrations and examples of what I had in mind. Indeed, it seemed to me that examples tended to mislead readers who focus on the images and their associations and fail to consider the conceptual point illustrated. This ability of thought to move without recourse to mental images from an initial transition or shift through reflection on what has gone on to new, unified thought, I suggested, underlies the "systematic" development of Hegel's *Science of Logic*.[7]

Not surprising, I was soon attacked for having committed the fallacy of psychologism.[8] Logical argument, I had claimed, derived from psychological processes. But these, as subjective, cannot establish the

---

7 J.W. Burbidge, *On Hegel's Logic: Fragments of a Commentary* (Atlantic Highlands, NJ: Humanities, 1981).

8 George di Giovanni, "Burbidge and Hegel on the Logic," *Owl of Minerva* 14, no. 1 (Sept. 1982), 1–6.

objectivity required. For logic, the objection reminded me, concerned itself with validity. And that does not depend on what any particular person happens to be thinking. Whenever Hegel shows how one concept leads on to another, he claims that it is the very meaning of the concept itself that requires the transition, even if no one has ever actually thought the concept in that form before. To base logic on various kinds of psychological activity – transitions, reflection, conceiving – is to dissolve that reliable universality; logic, far from emerging from what people actually think, rather sets the standard against which to measure their individual successes or failures. Any logic worth its salt must be true, irrespective of whatever happens in the world of physical events and human experience. If we cannot rely on the absolute reliability of logic's structure, we have no basis for determining whether we are progressing or regressing in our understanding of the changing world in which we live.

The charge is serious. When human beings think, there is no guarantee that they will all end up with the same conclusions, even when they start from the same premises. I recall, for example, the mature student in my introductory logic class, who had already produced an Academy Award–winning short film. He was adept at intuiting the relationship between a number of visual scenes and situations, and he started confidently into the first exercise, which involved distinguishing arguments from other forms of rhetorical expression. When we sat down to discuss the answers, however, it turned out that his answers ran directly counter to the conventional claims of the logical texts. Whatever the dominant tradition thought to be arguments he thought simply digressions. And those passages it claimed involved rhetorical persuasion he identified as arguments. Moreover, I could not convince him that he was wrong. Perhaps he brought a different context to his reading of the selected passages from that which logically precise thinkers adopt. Perhaps the academic discipline isolated the passage from any assumed context, whereas he intuited connections to all kinds of related meanings. In any case, it was clear that his mind did not make the same moves as mine – that his thinking followed a different pattern. The logician in me wanted to claim that only strict reliance on the meaning of the terms directly involved – such as "because" and "therefore" – was appropriate to the assignment. If one does not hold to that fundamental "objectivity," I wanted to say, then there can be no basis for deciding between reliable and unreliable conclusions. But in making that response, I could no longer appeal to the transitions of pure thought, but had to rely on some standard against which to assess such thinking.

A quick response to this story is that the mature student was working with representations and ideas, whereas logicians work with concepts. He was drawing on intuitions, associations, and the play of creative imagination in making his decisions. The logician, in contrast, relies simply on the abstract meanings of such terms as "since," "as a result," and "hence" and on their implicit presence in other passages. The sense of these concepts is not a function of what actually goes on in anyone's mind. It is independent and universally valid, in any culture and in any context. Indeed, it continues to hold even if there were no people to think it at all. It is as if we humans once "discovered" that meaning sometime in our evolutionary history, in the same way that Europeans "discovered" the Americas in the fifteenth century; it is not something that we generate out of the way our minds happen to operate.

So I could not lightly dismiss the critic's charge of psychologism against my interpretive framework. The distinction between ideas and concepts is fundamental to the development of modern logic. And even though it is difficult, if not impossible, to translate Hegel's massive and incomprehensible text into the formulae and conventions of contemporary logical discussions, whether symbolic or informal, there can be no doubt that Hegel intended his logic to set an objective standard against which to measure all the rest of philosophy – indeed all reflective thought. If the interpretive thread that I had used to decipher his prose implied that the systematic development was a function of the way certain people happen to think, then it could not do justice to what Hegel was about.

So we must return to Frege's sharp dichotomy between ideas and concepts. The relative success of my interpretive thread makes me reluctant to abandon all reference to the processes of conceptual thinking. However, the evident relativity that marks the way people actually use their minds, and the independence of such disciplines as mathematics and theoretical physics from the intellectual processes of their practitioners in reaching their conclusions, make Frege's conclusions hard to avoid. So, in an attempt to resolve this tension, this study explores the relations between ideas and concepts to see how they differ and how they both can function none the less within a single human mind.

It raises a number of questions: Can one ever try to understand the logic of concepts by appealing to the activity of thinking – of conceiving? Indeed, what is the relationship between the noun "concept" and the verb "conceive"? If concepts have some kind of independent subsistence, beyond the realm of normal human experience, how is it possible that we can on occasion apprehend them and examine them for their implications and interconnections? If, however, concepts really are the product of a human activity we might call "conceiving," how do they acquire their normative role when the human mind assesses valid and invalid inferences and acquires knowledge of the world? How can human initiatives – despite the obstacles of subjective distortion and personal interest – ever become refined enough to reach universal truths?

Once we raise these questions, they spill over into a wide range of current debates in the academy. On one extreme are people who claim that all reasoning is human and so subjective: there are no universal truths; each position, even when established by the most disciplined scientist, simply reflects the context and conditioning of the investigator. On the other extreme, most mathematicians and scientists affirm that it is only by relying on the strict objectivity of mathematical concepts that they can reach definitive conclusions about the nature of reality – of the cosmos, of the smallest particles, of geological formations, of biological development, and indeed of social and economic life. In between, the discussion of concepts and ideas is central to epistemology, the philosophy of language, the philosophy of logic, and even the philosophy of mind.

The critical question is how to proceed. Rather than presuming a position of authority from which to assess theories, both past and present, it is useful to enter into dialogue with those thinkers who have reflected on similar questions and proposed subtle and well–thought out answers. We can learn from their insights, even as we recognize their limitations. So, in the pages that follow, we encounter Plato, Aristotle, the Stoics, Descartes, Locke, Berkeley, Hume, Kant, Hegel, J.S. Mill, C.S. Peirce, and Frege. I introduce each at the point where his thoughts can contribute to our itinerary.

Our initial question structures the first part of that itinerary: how are ideas related to concepts? Frege sets the stage in chapter 1, with his challenge to "psychologism." In chapter 2, I consider how the British empiricists reduce human understanding to the way ideas are formed from our sensations and experiences. Hegel then offers us – see chapter 3 – a psychology describing how we move from such ideas to abstract thoughts – through language (chapter 4) and memory (chapter 5). Since pure thoughts remain ambiguous, we turn in chapter 6 to Descartes to propose a way forward and apply in chapters 7, 8, and 9 his second, third, and fourth rules of reasoning, with the assistance of Aristotle, Kant, and Peirce. Chapter 10 draws out the implications of this analysis for our understanding of concepts.

Having in part I shown how concepts can emerge from psychological operations, I explore in part II some implications that follow from that discussion. In chapter 11, I return to Hegel to explore what happens when we conceive; Hegel's "indeterminate" terms offer implicit meanings – I call them "tendrils" – that lead eventually to more fully refined concepts. Next, I see how traditional forms of inference can help us explore these tendrils and how they connect concepts: Aristotle's syllogisms (chapter 12), *modus ponens* (chapter 13), and arguments from analogy (chapter 14). In chapter 15, I suggest that the syntax of a language can influence the kinds of tendrils that a reflective thinker might explore. And in chapter 16, I draw conclusions about how ideas and concepts interact in our daily lives. An Epilogue suggests some metaphysical implications of the arguments of this volume.

For concepts turn out to be not isolated, independent, and unchanging atoms of meaning, but contain tendrils that reach out towards other meanings and alter their sense as we explore those implications.

If this argument is successful, then, we will not need to follow Frege in placing ideas and concepts in two different realms, one in the human mind and the other in a Platonic heaven. The various functions of the human mind can build on each other, enabling us to escape our subjective and idiosyncratic world, to reach reliable conclusions about the way the world really is, and to act effectively in achieving our purposes. The following pages suggest how that is possible.

PART ONE

From Ideas to Concepts

1

Frege and Psychologism

WE START WITH GOTTLOB FREGE, who originally identified the fallacy of psychologism. What does he mean by the term? And what reasons does he give for labelling it a fallacy? Any solution to those questions can come only from a careful examination of his arguments.

Taking his stand against the introspective psychology of the nineteenth century exemplified by Mill and Husserl, Frege distinguishes "between image and concept, between imagination and thought."[1] As a general term for image and imagination, as well as "sensations" and "mental pictures, formed from the amalgamated traces of earlier sense impressions,"[2] Frege adopts the term *Vorstellung*, which his English translators render as "idea." For concept and thought, he uses *Begriff* and *Denken*, respectively, regularly translated as "concept" and "thought."

As Frege sees it, the problem with *Vorstellungen,* or ideas, is that they are subjective. "A man never has somebody else's mental image, but

1 "Review of Husserl's *Philosophie der Arithmetik*" [317], reprinted in G. Frege, *Translations from the Philosophical Writings of Gottlob Frege,* ed. P. Geach and M. Black (Oxford: Blackwell, 1966), 79. In the light of this review, Husserl changed his approach to logic and mathematics and developed a critique of psychologism in the *Prolegomena* to his *Logical Investigations,* trans. J.N. Finlay (London: Routledge & Kegan Paul, 1970). Whereas Frege frames the conflict in terms of ideas and concepts, Husserl focuses on laws: "The *opposite of a law of nature,* as an empirically based rule regarding what is and occurs, *is not a normative law* or a prescription, but an *ideal law,* in the sense of one based purely on concepts, Ideas, purely conceived essences, and so not empirical" (I, §43, 106).

2 G. Frege, *The Foundations of Arithmetic* (1884), trans. J.L. Austin (New York: Harper, 1960), xvii.

only his own; and nobody even knows how far his image (say) of red agrees with somebody else's."[3] Often saturated with feeling, ideas are internal images, "arising from memories of sense impressions which I have had and acts, both internal and external, which I have performed." As a result, it is highly unlikely that two people will have the same idea, or *Vorstellung*, for any term that they happen to use in conversation. "A painter, a horseman, and a zoologist will probably connect different ideas with the name 'Bucephalus.'"[4] Because "an idea in the subjective sense is what is governed by the laws of association; it is of a sensible, pictorial character;" and so on many occasions ideas are demonstrably different in different people.[5]

This is why Frege took his stand against using psychology to explain the rigours of logical reasoning:

The expression 'law of thought' tempts us into viewing these laws as governing thinking in the same way as the laws of nature govern events in the external world. They can be nothing other than psychological laws, since thinking is a mental process. And if logic were concerned with these psychological laws, then it would be a part of psychology. And so it is in fact conceived. These laws of thought can then be conceived as guiding principles in so far as they indicate a mean, just as we can say what counts as normal human digestion, grammatical speech, or fashionable dress. We can then only say: the *holding as true* [*Fürwahrhalten*] of things by people conforms on average with these laws, at present and to the best of our knowledge; if one therefore wants to remain in accordance with this mean, one will conform with them. But just as what is fashionable today ceases to be fashionable after a while and is not at present fashionable amongst the Chinese, so too the psychological laws of thought can only be laid down as authoritative with qualifications. This is certainly so if logic is concerned with *being held as true* [*Fürwahrhalten*] rather than with *being true* [*Wahrsein*]! And these are what the psychological logicians confuse ... In response I can only say: *being true* is quite different from *being held as true*, whether by one, or by many, or by all, and is in no way to be reduced to it. There is no contradiction in something

3 "Review of Husserl," 79.
4 "On Sense and Reference" [29], in G. Frege, *The Frege Reader*, ed. Michael Beaney (Oxford: Blackwell, 1997), 154.
5 *Foundations of Arithmetic*, 37.

being true which is held by everyone as false ... If being true is thus independent of being recognized as true by anyone, then the laws of truth are not
psychological laws, but boundary stones set in an eternal foundation, which
our thoughts can overflow but not dislodge.[6]

This sharp dichotomy between psychology and logic rules out any
investigation of logic as a function of some mental activity we might
call "thinking" or "conceiving." Then we would be in danger of defining as "good" those inferences and associations that appear common
within a certain society or setting. There can be no guarantee that we
are using our minds to reach reliable and true conclusions overall.

None the less Frege does not fall prey to the belief that all thinking
is relative. He distinguishes the subjectivity of *Vorstellungen*, or ideas,
from the objectivity of concepts and thought, *Begriffe und Denken*. In
a footnote to *The Foundations of Arithmetic*, he allows that in everyday
speech *Vorstellung* may include objects and concepts, both of which
are objective and not subjective, and so the same for all. In this sense,
"an idea in the objective sense belongs to logic and is in principle
non-sensible, although the word which means an objective idea is
often accompanied by a subjective idea, which nevertheless is not its
meaning."[7] But to avoid confusion, Frege limits his use of the term to
only its subjective sense.

So, in "On Sense and Reference" he distinguishes ideas (*Vorstellungen*)
from the sense of a sign, "which may be the common property of
many people, and so is not a part or a mode of the individual mind."[8]
Because "one and the same thought can be grasped by many men ...
the constituents of the thought, and *a fortiori* things themselves, must
be distinguished from the images that accompany in some minds the
act of grasping the thought – images that each man forms of things."[9]

Yet there is an interesting phrase in that last citation: "the act
of grasping the thought." Frege returns to it in a letter to Husserl:
"Thoughts are not mental entities, and thinking is not the mental
generation of such entities but the *grasping of thoughts* which are

6 *Grundgesetze der Arithmetik*, I, xv–xvi, in *Frege Reader*, ed. Beaney, 202–3.
7 *Foundations of Arithmetic*, 37.
8 [29], in *Frege Reader*, ed. Beaney, 154.
9 "Review of Husserl" [317], in *Writings*, ed. Geach and Black, 79.

already present objectively."[10] For all that concepts and ideas are objective and the same for everyone, human beings must use their minds if they are to apprehend them. "The grasp of a thought," Frege comments much later, "presupposes someone who grasps it, who thinks. He is the owner of the thinking, not of the thought. Although the thought does not belong with the contents of the thinker's consciousness, there must be something in his consciousness that is aimed at the thought."[11]

Throughout *The Foundations of Arithmetic*, Frege makes similar references to the intellectual dynamic involved in grasping a thought: "Often it is only after immense intellectual effort, which may have continued over centuries, that humanity at last succeeds in achieving knowledge of a concept in its pure form, in *stripping off the irrelevant accretions* which veil it from the eye of the mind." To define a concept requires a "*precise delimitation* of the extent of [its] validity." In an argument against Mill's thesis that numbers are the result of inductive generalizations, he writes: "The three in [a triangle] we do not see directly; rather we see something upon which we fasten an *intellectual activity of ours* leading to a judgement in which the number 3 occurs." "The concept," he goes on to say, with reference to Kant, "has a power of *collecting together* far superior to the unifying power of synthetic apperception." Not only do we acquire concepts "*by direct abstraction* from a number of objects. We can, on the contrary, arrive at a concept equally well by *starting from defining characteristics*; and in such a way it is possible for nothing to fall under it."[12]

So even if concepts are not subjective mental entities but have an independent existence apart from any mind that happens to think them, some kind of intellectual activity allows us to think them, an activity that can involve abstraction, construction, and some kind of collecting together. Indeed, at one point Frege suggests that one can improve this ability to grasp thoughts when one is able to dissociate oneself from the particular conditions of one's native language and from the associations and feelings that have attached to them: "It is true that we can express the same thought in different languages; but

---

10   In *Frege Reader*, ed. Beaney, 302 (my italics).
11   "Thought" [75], in ibid., 342.
12   *Foundations of Arithmetic*, xix, 1, 32, 61, 62 (my italics throughout).

the psychological trappings, the clothing of the thought, will often be different. This is why the learning of foreign languages is useful for one's logical education. Seeing that the same thought can be worded in different ways, we *learn better to distinguish* the verbal husk from the kernel with which, in any given language, it appears to be organically bound up. This is how the differences between languages can facilitate *our grasp* of what is logical."[13]

Because Frege refuses to identify the intellectual act of thinking (which would be psychological) with the content being thought, he has to distinguish between the act of conceiving and the concept apprehended. The latter is objective, stands in some sense outside the mind grasping it, and remains the same for all people who conceive it whenever and wherever that happens. It rises above the relativity that comes from idiosyncratic psychological traits, cultural differences, or historical development and resides in some Platonic realm of pure forms.[14] The mental activity is subjective, dependent on a particular person's intellectual development, and indeed the languages which she is able to speak or the cultures in which he lives; so it has nothing at all to do with logic.

But there is something peculiar about the distinction between the objectivity of concepts and the subjectivity of all intellectual activity. For what is it about the processes that go on in our minds while abstracting, collecting, and constructing our thoughts that enables us to move beyond our idiosyncrasies, so that we can eventually grasp in its completeness the sense of an independently subsisting concept and thus escape from the subjectivity of ideas and imaginative constructions? How are we able to free ourselves from our subjective experiences to understand and conceive pure, objective, concepts?

To indicate the relevance of these questions, let us look once again at *The Foundations of Arithmetic*, where Frege endeavours to define the

---

13 "Logic" [154], in *Frege Reader*, ed. Beaney, 243 (my italics). To be sure, even this approach may have flaws, so he goes on to argue for an artifical conceptual notation.

14 As a graduate student, I learned how this "objective" status of concepts posed problems for his empirically minded successors, who found it difficult to determine the ontological status of concepts or of any propositions that incorporated those concepts. They were reluctant to ascribe being or existence to entities that are neither spatial nor temporal, but eternal.

concept of number. He takes us through a whole sequence of arguments or reasonings, which involve rejecting the positions of other
thinkers, proposing alternatives, and justifying his final result as
something reliable and true. This train of reasoning appears to be in
some way significant for the conclusion he wants to reach; yet when
Bertrand Russell later showed that the definition Frege proposed results in a paradox of self-reference, the conceptual definition became
problematic. The intellectual activity in this whole process seems to
ensure that the concept we end up grasping is genuinely objective.
We benefit from knowing a number of languages; we follow through
implications and show that they lead to contradictions; we construct
solutions to apparent paradoxes; and we benefit from exposing the
flaws in our predecessors and contemporaries.

We reach the point where we think the pure, unchanging concept
through a psychological process that is not bedevilled by images and
associations, but rather struggles with the meanings of the concepts
themselves, even if, once we understand the concept, we "recognize" it
as holding for all times and places. It was Russell's "subjective" reasoning that showed how peculiar and idiosyncratic – indeed "psychological" – Frege's earlier definition had been. The divide between subjective
and objective does not seem to be as sharp as Frege suggests.

Once we notice that difficulty, we discover a subtle shift in Frege's
argument, which seldom attracts notice. He starts out by rejecting
ideas, or *Vorstellungen,* that derive from mental images and memories
and respond to the feelings and associations that emerge in idiosyncratic experience. He wants to avoid basing logical validity on the
psychological laws of association, which stem from such images and
memories. And since these were the objects of contemporary psychology, he identifies them with that discipline and so rejects them
under the blanket term "psychologism." But, as we saw above, intellectual activity includes more than the subjective mental imaginings
and *Vorstellungen* that were the initial object of concern. It also en-
compasses such mental acts as abstraction and construction, grasping
a thought, or understanding a meaning.

Calling the culprit "psychology," without restriction, conceals the
limited range of the phenomena that originally posed the problem
and expands the attack to include all intellectual acts whatever, even
those that do not obviously involve images, feelings, or associations.
It simply assumes that all such acts are the work of individual thinkers,

even when they arise in the disciplined search for mathematical or scientific truth; so they are in danger of becoming idiosyncratic. It ignores the significant differences between a stream of consciousness involving ideas, or *Vorstellungen*, and the mental discipline of conceptual understanding and inference, by which we refine our thoughts to ensure that they do justice to reality and can be understood by other people, even though both intellectual processes are functions of a single working intelligence.

In the light of these difficulties with Frege's formulation of the fallacy of psychologism, we need to do some more thinking about the various kinds of mental processes he discusses: specifically, the entertaining of ideas, or *Vorstellungen*, and the grasping of thoughts. How can they both be functions of a single human mind? And how are they to be distinguished so that, when we are thinking objectively, we are not afflicted by the temptations of our subjectivity? Frege's argument hinges on establishing a significant difference of kind between the two: one subjective, the other objective. What kind of mental activity introduces a break so radical that we can transcend our own limitations? Faced with this new set of questions, we might well go back to the British empiricists, who sought to explain logic by appealing to psychology, and see if the success or failure of their arguments might provide a way of proceeding.

2

From Sensations to Ideas: The Empiricists

THE BEST PLACE TO START EXPLORING what happens when we entertain ideas, or *Vorstellungen*, is with the British empiricists John Locke, George Berkeley, and David Hume. For they explicitly define ideas as retained images.

The seventeenth century saw vicious wars of religion. In Europe, the Thirty Years War set Protestants against Catholics. In Britain, the Civil War pitted High Church Anglican Royalists against Presbyterian and Independent Parliamentarians. These were conflicts not simply about power or control of land, but also about ideas and what people held to be true. Not surprising, then, the century also witnessed an interest in how to transcend mere opinion and achieve some confidence in our thinking. Is there a way we humans can dissolve conflicting beliefs into some kind of assured agreement?

On the continent, a mercenary soldier who had fought on both sides of the conflict, took respite from the battles and one day sat down by a warm stove to explore what conclusions he could reach if he relied only on indubitable convictions. By starting from clear and distinct ideas (or what we might call concepts), argued the mathematician, René Descartes, we can move towards reliable conclusions about the mind, God, and the world. We look at how he did this in due course.

In Britain, however, a different approach surfaced. As happened with Descartes, a dispute about religious matters started John Locke on the inquiry, which led to his *Essay Concerning Human Understanding*. But he was already highly suspicious of abstract principles or concepts. There was, he claimed, no evidence that humans immediately grasp such thoughts. Our minds start out, in effect, as blank slates, passively receiving both the input of our senses and the results of introspection on our internal feelings and functions. Copies of these immediate impressions (as Hume would later call them) become the ideas that eventually provide the constituents of our beliefs and knowledge. Every thought, then, ultimately derives, and acquires its justification, from an image impressed on the mind or from a combination of such images. To be sure, Locke allowed that we could isolate parts of such original images from their context and focus on them alone – a process he called "abstraction." But even so, what is important about ideas is no result of our mental activity but rather stems from our individual sensations, which we retain in our memory and then build into more complex constructions. By grounding our thoughts in our experience of the world rather than in the constructs of our minds, Locke maintained, we can reach reliable, and shared, conclusions.

In making this claim, Locke assumed that everyone's basic experiences, and the processes by which they become ideas, are essentially similar. He moved easily to a rather surprising affirmation: because of this shared internal dynamic, anyone who generates abstract ideas and then expresses them by some kind of signifying sound can easily establish linguistic communication with other sociable creatures. There is, however, an unexplained leap in this reasoning. All words, he says, even those that do not stand for sensible things, "have had their first rise from sensible ideas."[1] Thus "words in their primary or immediate signification, stand for nothing, but the ideas in the mind of him that uses them." Whenever the hearer "represents to himself other men's ideas, by some of his own, if he consent to give them the same names that other men do, 'tis still to his own ideas; to ideas that he has, and not to ideas that he has not."[2] None the less, Locke continues, people assume that their interlocutors also have ideas, signified by the same sounds, and *that the sounds stand for the same ideas.* This assumption is justifiable because "men would not be thought to talk barely of their own imaginations, but of things as they really are; therefore they often suppose their words to stand also for the reality

---

1 John Locke, *An Essay Concerning Human Understanding*, ed. Peter H. Nidditch (Oxford: Clarendon, 1975), III, i, §5. In all quotations from Locke, I abandon capitalizing his nouns, as well as his extensive use of italics.
2 Ibid., III, ii, §2.

of things."[3] But this justification contains two questionable assumptions: first, that our idiosyncratic sensations have direct acquaintance with what is significant in the real world, and, second, that people will generally make similar moves to the same "real" content even though they start from their distinct sensations and reflections.

Locke admits that the latter condition is not always satisfied. The fact that words "signify only men's peculiar ideas, and that by a perfectly arbitrary imposition, is evident, in that they often fail to excite in others (even that use the same language) the same ideas, we take them to be signs of." This problem makes all communication conditional and suspect: "Unless a man's words excite the same ideas in the hearer, which he makes them stand for in speaking, he does not speak intelligibly."[4] The reasoning sounds dangerously circular: the fact that people speak intelligibly shows that people talk of things as they really are; but it is because all words ultimately derive from immediate experience of the world that people can communicate effectively.

This places the critical step in his argument at the point where he claims that we can encounter things as they really are – that we can move beyond the idiosyncrasies of our immediate sensations and reflections. He realizes that circumstances condition many of our experiences. Colours and sounds can change depending on light and velocity; they are only secondary qualities. But, he maintains, there are primary qualities through which we have access to objects as they are in themselves: solidity, extension, figure, and mobility. The fragility of this move to objectivity becomes more explicit once Berkeley points out that our sensations of even the primary qualities of extension, shape, and mobility vary depending on the particular angle from which we approach a particular scene. The table we are looking at reveals not only a range of colours depending on how the light reflects off the surface, but also the shape of a trapezoid; its size varies depending on its distance from us. The sound coming from the vehicle on a busy road alters as it passes where we are standing. The shape of a sculpture we feel with our eyes closed is affected by the texture of its surface. The move from immediate impressions to ideas of things as they really are thus becomes increasingly problematic.

3 Ibid., §5.
4 Ibid., §8.

All our immediate sensations, which we receive passively, are conditioned by the timing and placing of our sense organs vis-à-vis the things that make their impression on them. We do not have unmediated access to solidity, extension, figure, and mobility. So it is not surprising that Immanuel Kant, following the empiricists in affirming our passivity when sensing, concludes that a spatial and temporal frame organizes these passive intuitions – a subjective space and time that is simply the universal form of all the data we receive. So the inevitable conclusion: in the pure receptivity of sensible intuition, we have access not to things as they really are but only to the way they appear from our restricted perspective. The move from (subjective) sensations to (objective) thoughts is impossible if we restrict ourselves to the pure receptivity of experience, but requires the active mediation of our minds.

Indeed, Locke appears to suggest this. We move beyond the particular qualities we are sensing to some idea of the thing in question only by using our minds to construct complex ideas. In other words, our idea of one thing, or of a substance that underlies a variety of direct sensations, is nothing but a supposition based on an (innate?) inability to imagine "how these simple ideas can subsist by themselves."[5]

In other words, because Locke rejects innate ideas, which would have to include any tendency of our minds to think in similar ways,[6] and because of the way he traces the origin of words and ideas back to the actual experiences of each individual, it is difficult to see how he can hope that two individuals will *ever* come to have *the same idea*. One begins to wonder why he believed that anyone else could correctly grasp the argument he puts forward in the *Essay*.

By basing the validity of ideas on our subjective and idiosyncratic experiences, then, Locke has set himself up for Frege's attack. If one bases all thinking on ideas deriving directly from personal experience, one cannot explain or justify the use of language to communicate common meanings. It is impossible to ensure that different

5 See *Essay*, II, xxiii, §1.
6 In Locke's discussion of complex ideas, he assumes that all human minds organize immediate sensations in regular ways, else he could not claim that such ideas stand for things as they really are. But this sounds as if he is bringing some form of innate ideas in by the back door.

minds are thinking the same thing, even though they may use the same word or sign.

This fundamental problem with Locke's analysis, however, did not prevent his successors from furthering his initiative. It was, for example, George Berkeley who saw the implications of Locke's theories for abstract ideas. There can be, for Berkeley, no such thing as a pure concept (if we use Frege's term) in a mind. Nor can minds abstract from the particular content of any retained image, as Locke suggests. Berkeley does not deny that people entertain general ideas. But these are simply a special application of the particular ideas deriving from immediate impressions. "Now if we will annex a meaning to our words," he writes, "and speak only of what we can conceive, I believe we shall acknowledge, that an idea, which considered in itself is particular, becomes general, by being made to represent or stand for all other particular ideas of the same sort."[7] Whenever we think of anything, what we have is a distinctive mental image, which stands as a placeholder for a number of associated sensations and impressions. Thinking the abstract noun "tree" involves perhaps picturing the apple tree that stood in our back yard when we were young. And that is the entire significance of the term, although we are ready to extend the image by analogy to oaks and maples, pines and poplars. It is only because we have used words to represent such ideas that philosophers have come to believe that there are such things as abstract ideas.

David Hume extended Locke and Berkeley's approach to a consideration of human reasoning more generally – the activity of minds. First, in *A Treatise of Human Nature* he introduced the distinction we have adopted above between impressions and ideas. Under *impressions*, "I comprehend all our sensations, passions and emotions, as they make their first appearance in the soul. By *ideas* I mean the faint image of these in thinking and reasoning."[8] These retained images

---

7 See in *A Treatise Concerning the Principles of Human Knowledge* (Indianapolis: Hackett, 1982), Introduction, §12, 13. As we can see from this passage, Berkeley does use the verb "conceive," but only to describe the entertaining of ideas or retained images.

8 D. Hume, *A Treatise of Human Nature* (London: Penguin, 1984), I, i, 1. Hume's use of the phrase "faint image" veils the complexity of the move from a particular direct sensation or feeling to the generality of an idea that applies to a number of experiences.

do not simply reflect what the person originally sensed, but become more general and are applied to other, similar experiences. Hume adopted from Berkeley the thesis that abstract, or general ideas are in fact particular images that have come to stand for a number of other similar images: "Abstract ideas are therefore in themselves individual, however they may become general in their representation. The image in the mind is only that of a particular object, tho' the application of it in our reasoning be the same, as if it were universal."[9]

At first, Hume claimed that, when the force or vivacity of the ideas increases, the mind moves from simply entertaining ideas or images to believing that objects really exist and have the characteristics that people associate with them as well.[10] By the time he had completed the third book of the *Treatise*, however, Hume had some second thoughts about this assertion: "Had I said, that two ideas of the same object can only be different by their different *feeling*, I should have been closer to the truth."[11] This suggests that belief in real existence is a matter of subjective feeling, not of any extra excitement deriving from the original impression. The tenuous connection that Locke sketched between particular sensations, thoughts of real things, and the generality of words is here being stretched to the breaking point. In other words, Hume agrees with Frege in pointing out that feelings radically infect retained images, which, like immediate sensations, vary from individual to individual.

Locke had said that the mind not only combines original impressions into more compound ideas – for example, taking the colour pink, the feeling of a thorn prick, and the smell of perfume into the compound idea of a rose – it also relates ideas to each other. Hume expands on this pattern of relation, calling it the action of reasoning: "Reasoning," he writes, "consists in nothing but a *comparison* and a discovery of those relations, either constant or inconstant, which two or more objects bear to each other."[12] A relation of this sort he defines as the "quality by which two ideas are connected together in

---

9 Ibid., I, i, 7. Earlier in the same chapter, he writes: "A great philosopher ... has asserted, that all general ideas are nothing but particular ones, annexed to a certain term, which gives them a more extensive signification, and makes them recall upon occasion other individuals which are similar to them."

10 See ibid., I, iii, 7.

11 *Treatise*, III, Appendix.

12 Ibid., I, iii, 2.

the imagination, and the one naturally introduces the other."[13] In other words, reasoning relies on natural connections that occur within
the stream of consciousness and that have developed over time from
repeated experiences of similar impressions, and the images that result from them. The philosopher or reflective thinker extends this
core competence and creates additional connections by comparing
ideas that the imagination arbitrarily brings together. Causation is the
only kind of reasoning by which the mind is "able to go beyond what is
immediately present to the senses, either to discover the real existence
or the relation of objects."[14] It, however, we can explain as the result of
"constant conjunction" – the repetition of similar experiences – and
the habits or customs of mind that this regularity generates.

The British empiricists start with sensations that can be compared
to notice how they are similar. As resemblances positively reinforce
each other, the mind retains an image of one that stands for all and
is retained as an idea – something general, now divorced from the
mind's immediate encounter with the world. Over time, experience
collects a number of such atomic ideas, which may then become units
in a further comparison, so it sees that the red of the rose (which
could be an initial general idea deriving from a number of direct
impressions) resembles the red of a cardinal and the red of a burning
cinder, which comes to stand as a sign for all of them, while the green
of its leaves comes to represent the green of a caterpillar and the
green of a patch of moss, or the sharpness of its thorn signifies the
sharpness of a needle and the sharpness of a mosquito bite. The process can extend further until the scarlet of these roses stands not only
for the common redness of a number of things, but also for the way
this red is like that green and the other blue, to form the general idea
of "colour"; and beyond this for the way colour is like other "qualities" of things: shape, taste, texture.

The whole process happens simply through what psychologists call
"positive reinforcement" – similar things repeated strengthen the
retained idea in the imagination and allow it to be compared with
other retained images, permitting the results to become ever more
general, until the image of this single flower may represent or stand
for a wide range of ideas, depending on what parts of that image are

13 Ibid., I, i, 5.
14 Ibid., I, iii, 2.

currently the focus of attention. Ultimately, each idea functions because the mind associates it with some image, or "decayed sense," which, as Berkeley says, continues to be its phenomenal existence – the face it presents to introspection. Reasoning is the residual work of comparison and resemblance.[15]

In the nineteenth century, John Stuart Mill further extended this empiricist tradition. After reiterating the principle that thoughts (or ideas) resemble sensations (or impressions) but have less intensity,[16] he then went on to develop the laws of association, advanced earlier by his father, James Mill, by which ideas retained subconsciously from the past may re-emerge, prompted by new impressions or other ideas already present in the mind. These laws are three in number. First, *similar* ideas tend to excite one another (Hume's relation of resemblance or identity). Second, when two impressions have *frequently* been experienced (or thought) either simultaneously or in immediate succession, then whenever one of these impressions, or the idea of it, recurs, it tends to excite the idea of the other (Hume's relations of space and time, together with his "constant conjunction"). And third, greater *intensity* in either or both of the impressions is equivalent, in rendering them excitable by one another, to a greater frequency of conjunction.[17]

Ultimately, all of Mill's laws and all of Hume's types of reasoning rely on the fundamental priority of the first: resemblance, or that similar

15 I deliberately avoid consideration of the more complicated mental process by which we move from particular qualities to clusters of them in the thought of things such as a rose, a garden, a palette, and so on.

16 *System of Logic*, VI, iv, §3, 557: "Whenever any state of consciousness has once been excited in us, no matter by what cause, an inferior degree of the same state of consciousness, or state of consciousness resembling the former, but inferior in intensity, is capable of being reproduced in us, without the presence of any such cause as excited it at first."

17 Ibid., VI, iv, §3. In his *An Examination of Sir William Hamilton's Philosophy*, Mill adds a fourth law: "When an association has acquired this character of inseparability – when the bond between the two ideas has been thus firmly riveted, not only does the idea called up by the association become in our consciousness, inseparable from the idea which suggested it, but the facts or phenomena answering to those ideas come at last to seem inseparable in existence." 2nd ed. (London: Longman's Green & Co., 1895), 191. This was to explain how we think of complex things that integrate a number of descriptive qualities.

ideas tend to excite one another. Because resemblance is a relation that derives from whatever the mind is comparing (whereas contiguity, simultaneity, and succession depend on the spatio-temporal setting of the agent who experiences), any reflective observer can recognize it about any kind of object. But, as we saw above, this ability to recognize similarity extends further back into the very formation of ideas. An immediate impression becomes an idea because it represents a number of other *similar* impressions. A particular idea becomes general when it comes to stand for other particular ideas *of the same sort*. The whole empiricist edifice presupposes the mind's ability to compare and to find similarities among retained images.

Resemblance is not as strong a claim as identity (although Hume sometimes uses that word). It allows that the ideas one is comparing may differ in some respects, for all that they are similar in those germane to the particular act of association. For the empiricists, the mind sets aside these differences so that the particular image can stand for the ideas it intends.

Despite what Hume claims, however, no two immediate experiences – even of the selfsame thing – are absolutely identical. As I suggested above, different perspectives and different lighting can change the visible characteristics of a sensation: the colour, the shape, the size. Texture and resistance can depend on which part of our body comes in contact with it and how. The sound of a train depends on whether it is approaching or moving away, whether it occurs in a muffled or a resonating environment.

This means that noticing resemblances in our experiences is not as straightforward and immediate as the empiricists suggest, even in the move from impression to idea. The latter is not simply a "faint image" of the former. We use our minds to discriminate and identify which feature of our sensory field we want to highlight in forming our simple, as well as our general ideas. So even at this most basic level, there is an act of abstraction; we focus on one particular aspect of our sensations rather than another. And this process of discrimination becomes more complicated as we move into more general contexts. Does the rose image in our minds represent a shade of pink, or a shade of green; things which can prick, or a particular perfume; a particular species, or roses in general; garden plants, plants as opposed to animals, or all living things; the advent of summer, or Romeo's love for Juliet? The initial image by itself, which is all that results from our immediate impression, does not tell us what content we are to think.

The further one moves from the concrete, the more arbitrary does this process of noticing resemblances become. At the most basic level, we must decide whether we are thinking of red, a rose, a flower, or a shrub. When we come to Hume's customary sequences, are we to think of how day follows night, how particular images of our house follow one another as we walk around it, or of how thriving plants follow rain showers? If a friend tries to explain what the word "walk" means by moving from his chair to the door, we may have difficulty in knowing whether he wants us to think of "exiting," "moving," "restlessness," or "exercise." And if this conversation takes place while we are already walking, and he walks faster to make his point, can we be sure that the term does not refer to "running."[18]

The fact that similar sensations frequently recur in our experience provides some justification for the empiricist claim that the world of ideas, or *Vorstellungen*, is a function of our ability to notice resemblances and generalize. Comparison emerges at a number of different levels, starting with the simple shift to a primitive image, through an ascending hierarchy to the most general of causal connections. None the less, it remains in thrall to the basic problem of all appeals to direct experience that Frege identifies: spatial and temporal context shapes immediate impressions, which fit into the stream of each person's unique consciousness; interests and feelings influence them; and comparison identifies similarities through a mental operation separate from the concrete details. And since we must not appeal to any innate ideas, there is no obvious reason to assume that all people will perform those operations in the same way, whether in forming the most basic ideas or in making the generalizations that emerge. Ideas whose only justification involves an appeal to immediate experience cannot hope to provide a reliable measure for public communication, much less arrive at some valid knowledge of the world beyond our direct acquaintance.

There are, then, more sophisticated operations involved in moving from impression to idea than simply noticing resemblances in an

---

18 This last example comes from Augustine's dialogue: *De Magistro* or *The Teacher*. It appears in *Augustine: Earlier Writings*, trans. J.H.S. Burleigh (Philadelphia: Westminster, 1953), 69–101.

immediate and direct way. Even the formation of the simplest ideas presupposes kinds of mental activity other than comparison, such as abstraction and discrimination. To gain some sense of what these might be and how they function, we need to look more closely at what happens to the immediate sensations and impressions of direct experience as the mind incorporates them into the dynamic spontaneity of mental activity. By identifying what operations, other than simple comparison, come into play, we may be able to develop a more accurate picture, not only of the way we come to share a common language, but also of how we achieve reliable thoughts about the world. We need to overcome the fundamental lacunae we have identified in Locke's argument and in those of his successors.

3

How Ideas Emerge: Hegel

WHAT INTELLECTUAL OPERATIONS are involved in formulating ideas? What happens as we develop internal images from immediate sensations to the point of using language? In the psychology of Georg Wilhelm Friedrich Hegel, I found a fairly detailed analysis of that process – one more plausible than the empiricists'. By using his text as a guide,[1] one can develop a narrative describing how distinct intellectual functions emerge, each building on the one that precedes, and setting the context for what follows. As each one surfaces in the story, I highlight it, using italics.

We can start from what Hume calls the *impressions* presented by both the senses and internal reflection. Since we receive these passively, we have the conviction that we are in direct contact with reality. But these immediate sensations are not atomic, isolated units, each one arriving in independent isolation, but a rich panorama of sights, sounds, textures, smells, and feelings. They change constantly; for time presses forward, and we move from place to place. Indeed, when we abstain from any initiative on our part and simply immerse ourselves in what is happening, we find ourselves in a flowing stream that can soon become a chaos of varying and mutating impressions. Since these impressions simply appear, there is nothing that separates or distinguishes them from each other.

For this multitude of sensations and impressions to develop some significance requires more than simple, passive reception. We need to take some initiative. From within the wide range of sights and

1 See G.W.F. Hegel, *Philosophy of Mind*, trans. W. Wallace and A.V. Miller (Oxford: Clarendon Press, 1971), §§445–60, 188–218.

sounds, textures and smells, we *focus our attention* on particular givens and take note of how they differ from their surroundings. We individuate them through conscious activity that shines its spotlight on some moments and lets others slip into oblivion.

Empiricist literature talks as if the primary items of our immediate awareness are undifferentiated blocks of colour, distinctive shapes, and, possibly, insistent sounds. It seems more likely, however, that what attracts our attention is not things that are static and uniform, but changes and alterations: perhaps a bird song that erupts from a nearby tree, the mauve light that appears as the sun sets, the nervous sprint of a chipmunk. Movement attracts our notice and leads us to focus on what has moved. The sensations that are to become the basis of our cognitive treasury, then, are not of simple qualities, but of actions, events, and whatever constitutes them.

By focusing on some of the givens of sense and reflection, we separate them off from the multi-faceted panorama that the senses provide and appropriate them into the domain of our minds. We select particular changes and entities from the flowing stream of immediate experience and make them our possession. We have looked into, or *intuited,* some of the givens that have impressed themselves on our mind.

But these intuitions do not stay long. Other experiences press upon us, and we turn to new sounds, new sights, new feelings. When we are no longer aware of them, however, the original intuitions do not evaporate into nothingness. Once they have become our possession through the focus of attention, they *disappear into a hidden part of our minds* that retains impressions even though we are no longer conscious of them. At the time, certainly, we do not notice this archiving activity. But later, long after our first encounter with the fragrance of a pink rose, for example, we run into another rose; and the retained image of the first pops back into our mind. We can *recollect* that initial encounter only because, once it happened, the "dark pit" of our subconscious absorbed it as part of its inventory. Because the initial spotlight of our attention made it our own, our intellect is able to store it somewhere separate from the cinema of our conscious life.

In the act of recollection, we recall an original intuition because our new experience reminds us of it; we are directly aware that one resembles the other. As that kind of experience continues to repeat itself, the original retained image comes to *represent, or stand for,* what is common among all the occurrences; it becomes the idea or representation

(*Vorstellung*) of "pink rose." In Hume's language, we have moved from our original impression to its idea. But, despite what Hume says, this idea is not simply a pale copy of the original. It also stands for the way the original resembles other similar intuitions, and it draws on the increasing store of past experiences that, over time, have disappeared into the "dark pit" of our subconscious. We have moved from a singular image or intuition to something more general.

This general schema allows for at least three types of variations. First, the "image" need not be visual. It could be a particular perfume or taste. It could be the rustle of leaves in the wind or the song of a sparrow. It could be the texture of a petal, the prick of a thorn, or the felt shape of a leaf. Any one of them could represent, or stand for, what is common to the original and the current impression.

Second, the image represents more than a particular perspective or sensed quality that happens to recur. The mind collates a number of impressions of a single rose to form a more general image. Some of these were part of the continuum of sensations that initially occurred as we moved towards and around a particular place. But others are simply possibles. We have a sense of the object as three-dimensional, with a past and a future; we can anticipate perspectives and sensations that have not in fact happened in our experience.

Third, a particular image can come to stand for a number of different generals, for it resembles not only pink roses, but also rose gardens, flowers in general, plants with thorns, even vegetable nature as distinct from animals. In other words, the one image can represent a range of ideas, from the particular to the abstract.

To this point, we have already identified three distinct mental initiatives in the formation of ideas, some conscious and some not: intuition, with its focus of attention; the storing of impressions in our subconscious; and recollection, which draws on that subconscious to transform the particular image into something more general by using singular, recalled impressions to represent similarities. But this is not the end of the process. As both Hume and Mill recognize, the mind relates ideas to one another – compares them within a single, attentive moment. Since ideas are, at this point, nothing but retained images – we call this synthetic operation *imagination*. This function, however, is not homogeneous and uniform, but assembles and relates mental pictures in various ways.

At first, the imagination operates almost instinctively. We simply find images connected one to another in our minds, usually because of some feature present in the original intuitions. At one time, we notice a rose in a garden, along with the singing of birds and the shade of a giant elm. So the image of a rose brings with it the recollection of a sparrow's trill or the pleasure of a cool moment on a hot day. *Contiguity of space and time* Hume calls this kind of association.

Or, each time we saw a rose and tried to pick it, a thorn pricked us. And that *constant repetition* links the idea of a pricking with that of a rose.

Or we notice that the red of a rose *resembles* the red of our blood, or the red of a fire engine.

The "stream of consciousness" thus wanders through a whole paradise of related thoughts, leading us far away from where we began. This chain, says Hegel, is the result of the kind of *imagination that reproduces* experiences from the past. As in the formation of ideas, this reproductive imagination builds on resemblances; but now these are not between repeated instances of similar things, but rather resemblances we notice in the experienced environment of things and events, by which we link them to other things and events. They are, in other words, resemblances of relation; and they enable our minds to extend its range beyond what we immediately sense to connections far removed from where we began.

We can divorce the relation, too, from its original context and apply it to other ideas. A pink rose that we see in a hospital ward may lead our thoughts back to the sound of birds in a garden, and on to the musical soundscape that we experienced on a spring morning in a woodland park, a strenuous climb up a mountainous path, the glorious vision from the top, the heat of the sun, and finally the sand on an open beach. Sherlock Holmes exploits such streams of consciousness to surprise Dr Watson by responding to a question just in the process of being formed within the latter's mind. The reproductive imagination moves beyond the given to new ideas that link together in unanticipated ways the items stored in the subconscious treasury of ideas and images.[2] So, as experience accumulates, an original image comes to stand for a diversity of ideas.

---

2 Dreams, as the work of this subconscious, create all kinds of association that seem far removed from anything in our conscious past. So there may be many more sorts of association than those that Hume and Mill enumerate.

The work of imagination need not be simply reproductive – the passive, almost instinctive, effect of our original experiences. It may also be the product of our active, though subconscious, minds; so, if we want, we can assume control of this activity and manipulate it deliberately. We then use our imaginative skills to create connections that have never before been part of our experience, bringing together ideas in novel and unpredictable ways. We formulate metaphors; we generate fantasies; we write poetry; we construct castles in Spain. This use of *fantasy* is where the mind's creative freedom first makes its appearance, and we begin to assume responsibility for our own possessions. Rather than simply responding to the determinate features of images we retain from our experience, we now generate new kinds of images and new kinds of relations. A red rose, we say, is like our beloved. So we explore similarities that are not obvious; we see the world in a different light; and we discover ways of imagining or thinking about possible worlds quite unrelated to the one in which we live. The realm of possibilities has expanded to include relationships that have never occurred before.

Hegel suggests, however, that we have a third type of imagination in addition to reproductive association and fantasy. As we establish more control over the working of our own minds, we may become reflective and focus our attention on the similarities and resemblances which we have been using to link ideas and create imaginative syntheses. Up to now, whenever we brought these to mind, we simply adopted one of our retained images and let it stand for the noticed resemblance.[3] The original pink rose we recollect stands for all roses whenever we encounter or think of them. But it may also represent lots of other events and entities – the colour pink, the pricking of thorns, flowers set out in gardens, the smelling of a pleasant perfume, our graduation ceremony, our paramour. This ambiguity easily generates confusion and imprecision. Initially, we focused on just one aspect or another of the retained image, and ignored for the time being all the others. Ranging through the diverse foci of our attention, however, we do not find it easy to discriminate clearly among the scores of possibilities. It would be more convenient if we could distinguish among these various uses of the pink rose image in our mind in more permanent and reliable ways. Imagination responds to

3 Much in the manner Berkeley suggests.

this challenge by introducing a variety of signs, using each one to represent a single kind of resemblance. We could draw pictures – but icons turn out to be as ambiguous as the original, retained image. More effective is the use of arbitrary patterns of sounds, where we can make each pattern quite distinctive and require no past association to link the sign with what we want to represent. These spoken words are the work of the third imaginative activity we may call *sign-making imagination*.

At first, each word is simply a pointer that directs our mind to a particular idea – some retained image that we view from a single perspective. It does not, however, name either the image or the event it pictures, but rather isolates one of the many possible resemblances that it has opened up in our minds. As such, all words are general. Even proper names signify the variety of different occasions we have encountered (or heard about) Albert Einstein, explored or read about Paris, appealed to the Declaration of Human Rights. The value of language lies in its ability to distinguish between different general relationships or resemblances, by abstracting from the concrete complexity of singular experiences and individual images and ideas. This discriminating activity builds on our mind's native ability to notice similarities among events and things, first evident in recollection, but expanded through the dynamics of imagination.[4]

With this description of the way language emerges in an individual mind, we pause in our narrative. We have been following the steps that Hegel identified in his psychology. We have isolated and demarcated distinct functions, not in the sense that they are absolutely independent of each other, nor that they need occur in just this order. Rather we have explored a plausible sequence, in which we can see how each operation, familiar from our own experience, builds on, and presupposes, what precedes.

In this story, we have identified a number of intellectual functions, central to the formation of ideas, or *Vorstellungen*: *intuition*, with its focus of attention; the *storing* of impressions in the subconscious; *recollection*, which draws on this dark treasury; *using images* to represent

---

4 There is nothing distinctively human about this capacity, as animal psychologists have demonstrated.

similarities; *reproductive imagination,* with its innate ability to associate ideas on the basis of similarity, contiguity, repetition, and intensity; the *creative imagination* and its generation of metaphor, poetry, and fantasy; and, finally, *sign-making imagination,* in which we create devices for representing particular resemblances and distinguishing them from other, closely related, ones.

In doing so, we have been following the British empiricists, as they traced the development of language from impressions and ideas. But we have discovered that it is a more intricate growth than they originally suggested. The mind is not nearly as passive as John Locke had claimed. It focuses its attention; it retains experiences in the subconscious; it recollects; it instinctively recognizes similarities; it draws associations and creates new metaphors; it signifies and distinguishes particular resemblances by creating words. Some of these basic skills are almost instinctive, others are deliberate and arbitrary. All are amenable to wider use – we need not apply them just to the retained images in the storehouse of our memory. But what those uses are will emerge only as we proceed.

There is, however, one important characteristic that limits the range of this narrative. It traces a development through the workings of a single intellect – as if it all happens within one human mind. Recollection can build on the specific intuitions of only a single individual. The "laws of association" are a function of the experiences that have become embedded in a particular subconscious. The creative imagination is the work of a unique inventive mind. And as I have described it, we adopt signs simply to distinguish among our own ideas. In other words, the ideas and representations we have been talking about are all prey to the difficulty Frege identified: "A painter, a horseman, and a zoologist will probably connect different ideas with the name 'Bucephalus.'"[5] No two people can ever share the same mental picture, or the same association.

So there is a gap in our description. We have talked as if the individual mind, having noticed and created similarities, generates distinctive signs for each of its ideas independently – entirely on its own initiative and for its own purposes. But that is never the case. Language is not simply a means of expressing our own ideas; it is also a means

---

5 "On Sense and Reference" [29], in *Frege Reader,* ed. Beaney, 154.

of communication. We use signs to inform others of what is going on in our minds – to draw distinctions between this significance of the pink rose and that one. This can happen because the signs we use are not self-generated, not simply the product of our own creative imagination, but are appropriated from the vocabulary of our culture. Through language, we not only discriminate among our immediate ideas, but also overcome the isolation of uniquely private experiences. This, however, raises the next question to explore. How is it that words function, not as private possessions, but as a public language?

4

Language

LANGUAGE IS A COMMUNAL, not an individual, accomplishment. Each person is not alone in recollecting images out of the dark pit of the subconscious, in using them to represent shared features, in finding the mind wandering along the pathways of association, in generating metaphors and fantasies, and in creating signs to stand for particular resemblances and meanings. We are born into a community that already gives voice to its thoughts and understands what others say. In one sense, each sign is arbitrary, since no idea requires a particular set of sounds as its sign. None the less we do not freely choose the syllables we adopt, but take them over from our family, friends, and acquaintances.

The fact that we are able to communicate one with another, however ineffectively, tells us that our ideas are not condemned to reflecting nothing more than our own isolated perspective. As we become competent in speaking a language, we gradually modify our ideas. No longer do they reflect simply the particular resemblances and generalities that happened to occur within our experience or emerge from our subconscious. We now have two or more speakers, each with a distinctive intellectual history – a variety of experiences, reactions, interests, and activities. Through the use of signs and language, each reaches beyond his or her peculiar isolation. This reciprocal give-and-take generates a new kind of arena for mental activity – one no longer located within a particular human organism, but somehow dwelling in the space between.

Here again, Hegel provides a helpful way of characterizing what happens in this interaction. Early in his chapter on self-consciousness in the *Phenomenology of Spirit* occurs a brief, rather abstract analysis of a process he calls "recognition" or "acknowledgment." It consists of three distinct components.[1] First, when two self-conscious individuals meet, they initially become aware of their basic similarity; they are not as unique as they had thought. Second, and in reaction, they affirm their distinct identities by stressing their differences. Then, third, they realize that they are the same in wanting to assert their uniqueness, yet even in their similarity they bring different perspectives. This dynamic is initiated from both sides, for the reactions of one stimulate the actions of the other. Because of this reciprocity, the effects accumulate, expanding both the ways in which the two are similar and the ways they differ. The result is an interplay of forces that develops a character of its own.

In an early manuscript, Hegel suggests that this pattern of recognition bridges the gap between the simple potential of our sign-making imagination and the reality of language as it exists in a people or nation.[2] Within our lived experience, in other words, the dynamic interplay of action and response provides the medium within which language functions. We develop our linguistic skills not in isolation, but through a dynamic process of recognition in which we discover how we are similar to, yet different from, our fellows. Thus the story Hegel tells can throw light on how we move beyond the idiosyncrasy of our own ideas to a world of shared speech.

Consider what happens when we enter a strange environment. As experience accumulates and we notice parallels to more familiar contexts, we identify significant patterns of resemblance, possibly associating particular images with each one. Then we turn to our fellows. We describe what we are seeing, using a familiar vocabulary, drawing on parallels and analogies. They, however, have adopted different sets of terms. On the one hand, we all know that we are interacting with the same context; on the other hand, each of us has drawn on the particular background of his or her mental history. Using a basic core of common terms with fairly conventional meanings, we explore

1 See G.W.F. Hegel, *Phenomenology of Spirit*, trans. A. Miller (Oxford: Clarendon, 1977), §178–84, 111–12. In fact, he has four stages, since he describes the first three from the perspective of only one of the participants, and the fourth points out that it happens from both sides.

2 See G.W.F. Hegel, *Gesammelte Werke* (Hamburg: Meiner, 1975), Band 6, Fragments 20 and 22.

the reasons for our differences and in the process discover welcome perspectives we had never noticed, common insights underlying our various interpretations, and the perversity and idiosyncrasy of some of our associations. As we gradually take account of others' experiences, we refine our vocabularies so that they approximate each other, and we learn to use common meanings to indicate how our perspectives differ.

In the course of this development, the triple pattern of recognition is active in four ways. On the first, most basic level, we start by realizing that we share the ability to use signs to represent or signify our ideas. We desire, in reaction, to capture what is unique to our own experience as distinct from theirs. In doing so, we discover that we can easily adapt common signs to articulate particular interests.

The same dynamic recurs at a second level, of content. We start out by assuming that everyone means the same thing by the same sign; we all share the same basic set of images and ideas. When we discover that this is not so, we retreat to our own world, claiming that our thoughts are ineffable, so unique that there are no public signs that can do justice to them. But even this denial uses the conventions of speech to distinguish shared meanings from idiosyncratic associations; and it struggles to identify those features that separate what is ours from what is theirs. As the self-conscious use of conventional language expands, we discriminate ever more clearly between what is uniquely our own and what is common, by showing how they contrast and interconnect.

When we assume, in the third place, that other people are telling the truth, only to learn that they are being polite, flattering us, or simply lying, we follow the same rhythm; we move to always taking what they say with a grain of salt until we have some independent corroboration of its reliability.

When, in the fourth place, we first encounter people speaking a different language, we may initially think that they should be able to understand us; next assume that they are particularly obtuse because they do not; and ultimately realize that they are using different signs for meanings that we none the less share. In other words, our ability to communicate with each other through words and signs incorporates a rich diversity of interactions, all of which betray the triple dynamic of shared identities, of contrasting differentiation, and of cooperative interaction.

Examples are easy to come by. I tell a three-year-old that I saw a deer fly; "Deer don't fly," he replies; the same expression turns out to have at least two, quite distinct senses. In an early draft of this chapter, I wrote "plethora" ("morbid condition; unhealthy repletion; oversupply") where I had wanted to talk of a rich multitude; the public term does not have my assumed meaning. I had grown up in eastern Canada, and was nonplussed when I heard an Albertan say that he was going to "pack a pail of water to the barn"; what I connected with putting things together into a bundle or box, he used for the act of carrying. Gilbert Ryle once admitted that neither German nor French has a word that captures just what he intended with the concept of "mind."

Thus the dynamic field of public speech incorporates at many levels the complex process Hegel calls "recognition." First, and at its most primitive, we discover that other individuals share the same capacity to create signs that we do, for all their different experiences and background. Then, second, we grasp the fact that, for some terms, we mean one thing while they mean something else. So, third, we adapt our vocabulary until we use the same sign for the same meaning. We come to see that other people have their own languages, with not only a different vocabulary, but different conventions for assembling signs into meaningful sentences.[3] The recognitive interplay between similarity and difference applies not only to the way we initially enter into the non-physical realm of social interaction, but also to how we acquire our mother tongue and learn alien languages.

As this rich network of intercommunication expands, it modifies and transforms our ideas. No longer do they simply stand for the resemblance that our subconscious instinctively presented to our conscious attention. We discover that some of those similarities are trivial and insignificant, while others, which we had overlooked, may be significant and useful. We overcome the idiosyncrasies of our unique experience and move to ideas that we can easily share. We organize our experience into patterns adopted from our culture. For all that we continue to draw on our past to flesh out the content of our ideas, we have adjusted and universalized their form.

---

3 In chapter 15 below, I suggest that the difference in syntax may have some effect on the way we develop explanations.

Our ability to use a shared language, or even communicate across linguistic boundaries, does not develop simply because we point at the same object, as Locke suggested in his discussion of the origin of language. Nor do our spoken signs name particular images that happen to attend the diverse ideas in the minds of the speakers. Words name not single objects, but generalities that objects share; and we adjust the range and limits of those general thoughts as we take note of undetected similarities and ignored differences. So it is that, through conversation and debate, the rough edges of idiosyncratic experience become smoothed down into a basic core of shared meaning. For all that each of us may draw on associations from our personal experience, there is none the less a common nucleus that enables us to understand one another.

It is worth pausing at this point to reflect on several implications of Hegel's analysis of recognition, for they reveal significant characteristics of our mental activities. First, we have not only the positive reinforcement of similarity and resemblance, but also the negative corrective of differentiation and divergence. Second, we have moved beyond linear causal sequences to reciprocal interactions that feed on participants' actions and reactions to produce distinctive "fields of force." Third, we discover that the signs we have adopted to express our ideas have an independent life of their own. In the rest of this chapter, we briefly consider each of these points in turn.

First, the British empiricists, and in particular David Hume, developed their analysis by appealing to resemblance and positive reinforcement. Ideas are simply pale *copies* of impressions; when an event *recurs* often enough it creates expectations of causal connection. In the previous chapter, I relied on that pattern to develop the roles of recollection and imagination: an image comes to stand for a number of similar experiences; resemblance and contiguity trigger imaginative associations; ideas and their signs represent generalities. But when we have nothing but such positive connections, ambiguity threatens. There is a wide range of similarities that we can apply to any immediate impression; and positive impulses can result in a diversity of outcomes. So we need to balance resemblance and positive reinforcement with discrimination and negative differentiation – by setting limits and boundaries.

We introduce arbitrary signs to *distinguish* among a variety of possible similarities, since a single retained image may "stand for" or "represent" a number of different associations and resemblances. Signs enable us to discriminate among those ambiguous associations; each sign comes to separate out a single relation or link – a single similarity. We discriminate among different aspects or features even as we recognize similarities. And a similar exploitation of differences in order to make our ideas more useful is fundamental to the way we acquire the ability to communicate with our fellows, learn our native tongue, and explore other languages.

Differentiation is a mental operation not reducible to the passive reception of immediate experiences. It involves comparison, noticing what is present in one case and what is missing in another. The mind considers two or more ideas that the subconscious throws up at once; and it confronts the fact that they are not the same, even though they share similar features. As a result, it adopts different signs that will do justice to their variety. Our ideas become diverse and are able to capture the diversity present in our experience much more effectively. For differentiation notices what is not there; it introduces negation – something that can never be the object of direct experience. It determines where we will not go, as well as where we will, and it sets limits to our use of a term. It is critical to developing our intellectual capacities.

Noticing similarities and drawing out differences are not two distinct and independent operations, however. Each relies on the contribution of the other. By distinguishing among similar thoughts, we delimit and clarify the particular resemblance in question. And by setting a range of different ideas within a common or shared setting, we see how they connect to each other as diverse components of a complex and integrated unity. Differentiation enables us to articulate details within the rich jumble of positive influences that affect our minds; by noticing affinities, we come on interconnections that relate distinct thoughts to each other. In sum, similarity and difference turn out to be two sides of a single, complex mental operation.

This double action becomes more significant when we turn to the social world of spoken communication. In our search for a common vocabulary, we have to distinguish between similar, yet distinct meanings. There are important differences between "plant" and "flower," between "rose" and "violet," between "stem" and "root." And by sorting out their boundaries, we communicate what we have in mind more effectively. As we delimit the application of our signs, our ideas come to resemble those of our friends and relations; and theirs become more like ours. Through differentiation, we reach some measure of common understanding. An adequate vocabulary builds not only on resemblance and positive reinforcement, but also on rigorous distinctions.

Second, we should not underestimate the significance of this reciprocal activity. It challenges the common prejudice that all causal processes are linear and sequential. Since the early days of the scientific revolution, when Galileo and Newton explored the laws of mechanics, and Hume and Kant grounded our belief in inexorable causation, people have generally assumed that every cause produces its effect, that effect then produces a further one, and so on into an indefinite future. But what Hegel identified in his analysis of recognition, and what we have discovered in the interaction of noticing resemblances and drawing distinctions, is a process of interaction where the initiatives on each side stimulate a response that feeds back into and modifies the original action, so that they mutually influence and are influenced by each other.

This mutual give-and-take can, in due course, settle into a pattern that develops a character of its own. The unity that emerges is then free to interact with its environment not merely as a collection of independent units, but as an integrated agent. For example, a linguistic community shares a language and then enters into dialogue with other cultures; or a family develops a cohesive life within its neighbourhood, a team plays its games in competition, an orchestra enchants an audience, or a nation reacts to invasion. The pattern of influence is not simply sequential, along a single line of cause and effect, but reciprocal, reinforcing mutual dependence and common initiatives. Hegel's analysis pictures two individuals encountering each other. When we multiply the number of interacting agents, however, we have a complex dynamic that defies simple analysis.

Reciprocal interaction plays a major role in much of our intellectual life. But biology as well has noticed this kind of mutual causality. Kant, in his *Critique of Judgment*, noticed that in an organism the various components, or organs, interact in reciprocal ways, each producing or causing the others; this mutual influence results in a single, integrated organic structure. And this pattern extends further through the process we call "symbiosis": lichens growing on a rock are not a single organism, but a fungus and an alga benefitting from each other's distinctive qualities.[4] Certain insects and certain plants require each other for each to survive. Reciprocity is not just an aberrant characteristic of some humans, but a significant counterpart to the pattern of linear causal sequences.

Third, when we turn back to our primary interest in the way we become adept in the use of a common language, we find that these two factors – the capacity for differentiation and the way reciprocal interaction generates new, integrated unities – combine to produce a distinctive kind of mental entity. Signs are no longer simply the way individuals represent their ideas. By acquiring a life of their own within a culture, they become words, modified by the way individuals use them, but none the less setting standards against which to measure use. They are the product of a wide-ranging network of interaction in which variations emerge, are rejected by some or adopted by others, become dominant or disappear. Over time, they develop some consistency, so that, while their significance may change, sometimes deliberately through the use of imaginative metaphors, they none the less retain a persisting core that individuals can appeal to – a core enshrined in our dictionaries.

When you think about it, words are peculiar entities. They are the product of the interaction of myriads of individuals. But they are not fixed, for their usage can be modified by extension to related applications or by restriction to a specific alternative among a number of synonyms. At the same time, individuals cannot manipulate them arbitrarily. Since they are critical for effective communication, they have a built-in resistance to change. For all that we require signs to

4 "The world is full of symbiosis – some of it obviously ancient. Lichens are the toughest of all living things, able to perch on baking, dead stones in deserts and feed on a moment's fortuitous dew. They are a collaboration between fungi and algae. Only when little fungoid caps appear at the time of reproduction is the nature of the deception revealed. Many corals have photosynthetic algae within their roots that feed the simple animal with important nutrients. Fungi nurture the roots of orchids. The stomachs of ruminants house a great, digestive soup of microorganisms that break down the cellulose of grass, and without which the animals would soon starve." Richard Fortey, *Life: An Unauthorised Biography* (London: Folio, 2008), 63.

discriminate among our ideas, the words that we adopt are independent of our particular purposes and interests. The products of both careful discrimination and reciprocal interaction, they have a life of their own. We discover that they play a critical role in the move from ideas to thoughts.

For the time being, however, we need draw only the conclusion of our present chapter. The use of signs is not the work of idiosyncratic intellects, but an activity we share with others. The communal use of language involves a dynamic that Hegel has called "recognition." In its briefest form, this involves four steps: we assume agreement, learn of our differences, acknowledge both similarity and difference, and then find a shared way of understanding how and why we disagree. Similarity and difference, resemblance and disagreement, interact in a productive and ongoing dynamic that, at each stage, reflects the preoccupations and interests of the participants. There is here no linear development. Instead, struggle, failure, and misadventure mingle with achievement, success, and progress. In any novel situation, it is not clear in advance which are the significant similarities, and which the relevant differences. That must be both discovered and created by the interplay of reciprocal forces that constitutes the field of human interaction.

5

From Retentive to Mechanical Memory

IN THE CHAPTER ON "IMAGINATION" IN HIS *Principles of Psychology*, William James cites research by Sir Francis Galton in the late nineteenth century. Exploring "the illumination, definition, and coloring" of mental images, Galton wrote a number of scientists, asking them to think of the breakfast table they had sat at that morning and describe the images in their mind.

To my astonishment I found that, *the great majority of the men of science to whom I first applied protested that mental imagery was unknown to them,* and they looked on me as fanciful and fantastic in supposing that the words 'mental imagery' really expressed what I believed everybody supposed them to mean. They had no more notion of its true nature than a color-blind man, who has not discerned his defect, has of the nature of color ...

On the other hand, when I spoke to persons whom I met in *general society,* I found an entirely different disposition to prevail. *Many men and a yet larger number of women,* and many *boys and girls, declared that they habitually saw mental imagery, and that it was perfectly distinct to them and full of color.*

Galton had discovered "that scientific men, as a class, have feeble powers of visual representation. There is no doubt whatever on [this] point, however it may be accounted for."[1] Indeed, one of Galton's

---

1   F. Galton, *Inquiries into Human Faculty and its Development* (London: Macmillan, 1883), 83–114. The discussion appears in William James's *Principles of Psychology* (New York: Henry Holt, 1890), Vol. II, Chapter xviii, 50ff. More recently, Allan Paivio has developed a theory of dual coding, which does not rely on James's language of "faculties." On this theory, verbal and non-verbal systems are alternative ways humans

scientists commented: "It is only by a figure of speech that I can describe my recollection of a scene as a 'mental image' which I can 'see' with my 'mind's eye.'" At the same time, as James reports, "A person whose visual imagination is strong finds it hard to understand how those who are without the faculty can think at all."[2]

To this point in our analysis, we have been proceeding as if the account provided by the British empiricists fully describes our intellectual activity: whenever people think of anything, they are visualizing the mental image of some concrete object that stands for, or represents, the particular thought in their mind. But Galton's evidence suggests that not all people's minds are replete with mental images or ideas; some use no pictures at all in their thinking, but simply work with meanings or significance. Among those who imagine easily, we find artists, novelists, and film directors; among those who rely instead on pure thoughts are mathematicians and physicists, whose researches lead them into the far reaches of abstraction.

Some cultures transmit the wisdom of the ages through folk tales that illustrate responsible behaviour; others enshrine it in abstract treatises that avoid concrete illustration. I find it difficult to describe an accident scene to the police or tell someone how to recognize a friend in a crowd; but I have friends who do not easily move from discussing an act of cheating to questions of justice and equity and become completely lost when we differentiate debt from deficit or explore the logic of the square root of minus one.

Thus we have to move beyond the assumptions of the British empiricists: that images we retain from our past experience animate all our thoughts and that all terms are simply names for types of such images. At the same time, there is no need to divide human beings into two distinct species unable to communicate with each other: those who imagine, and those who think. There are many who can manoeuvre in both spheres, moving from imagination to abstraction

---

represent events. For example, one can think of a tree by focusing on the word "tree" or by forming a mental image of a tree. The verbal and image systems connect and relate, for one can think of the mental image of the tree and then describe it in words or read or listen to words and then form a mental image. See Allan Paivio, *Mental Representations: A Dual Coding Approach* (Oxford: Oxford University Press, 1986).

2 In these two extremes, we have empirical evidence of the distinction that Hegel and Frege drew between ideas or representations and concepts, between *Vorstellungen* and *Begriffe*. Cf. Prologue above.

and back again without difficulty. Indeed, when Frege contrasts ideas
with concepts, he assumes that we have this double capacity. Our
minds do not simply follow a path of association in response to retained images. We are also able to grasp pure thoughts and understand their significance.

Our discussion of language has shown that we are able to move
beyond the idiosyncrasies of our retained images. In interaction with
our fellows, we learn to distinguish meanings we share from those
that are peculiar to our individual histories. Even though we may use
the same image to represent different characteristics, we have as-
signed distinct signs to each so that we are free to focus our attention
on one or the other. Despite Frege's remark,[3] it does not require
pure concepts on anybody's part for the artist and the cowboy, the
physicist and the jockey, to agree on what it means when someone
asks us to lead Bucephalus into the stable. We have adopted words
that stand for shared meanings, despite our various histories. We are
able to distinguish a tree from other plants, even if it does not closely
resemble the imagined apple tree in our family garden: a palm or
pine, for example. In other words, we easily work with generalities
despite the specific ideas in our minds and reach consensus even
though we may recall different images. Through language, our intellect is able to distinguish among similarities that are far more subtle
than the concrete pictures in our mind's eye.

This means that we have to introduce a new item into our inventory of mental entities. We started with immediate impressions, and
then moved to ideas. We restricted the use of this latter term to the
way a retained image stands for or represents a similarity or resemblance. But now we have ideas that are distinct, yet share the same
image; we identify them rather by a distinctive spoken (or written)
sign. We have already used "meanings"to name their specific sense –
what the signs signify.

It is worth our while to spend a bit of time reflecting on what meanings are. They have emerged out of our past experiences, for they are
similarities and resemblances that our subconscious minds notice and
now discriminate as distinct from each other. While their content has
derived from sensations and feelings, the need to avoid ambiguities

---

3 "A painter, a horseman, and a zoologist will probably connect different ideas
with the name 'Bucephalus.'" From "On Sense and Reference" [29], in *Frege Reader*,
ed. Beaney, 154.

and communicate with others has moulded their form. They have acquired boundaries; for all their idiosyncrasies, they focus on communal features. This transformation is the first step in abstracting our thoughts from the concrete world of our sensations. For all that the meanings draw on our experience, they are no longer simply pale copies, for our discriminating and differentiating minds have refined them.

But this does not take us as far as concepts. Many quite articulate people are not comfortable with the world of mathematics and philosophy and rely heavily on their ability to visualize what they are hearing. Many sages communicate their wisdom in simple parables. Poets and preachers know that metaphor can be a more effective way of disseminating an insight than philosophical argument. And we tend to celebrate writers who make the results of science and mathematics accessible to the general public. We need some further moves if we are to explain how some humans are able to function without any pictures in their minds. What new kinds of intellectual skill free us from the contingency of retained images and make possible the rigour of pure thoughts?

So far, I have been merely extending the British empiricists' account. Even though the path that emerges from Hegel's psychology introduces a number of operations – attention, recollection, imagination, and language – that complicate the passivity of direct sensation, it none the less seems to mesh with many people's experience and retains the plausibility of Locke's empiricism. But once we start talking about the transition from ideas to pure thoughts, we are moving into new territory. We have now introduced those abstract ideas that Berkeley so vigorously rejected. We are talking about terms that are not simply formed by our sensations, but have been transformed by our use of language. Yet we have not reached anything like the objectivity of Frege's concepts. We are in some kind of intermediate psychological stage, one where we are exploring not the empiricists' ideas, but something we might call "thoughts." Hegel, after all, suggests that thoughts provide an intermediate stage between concepts and ideas.[4] He also identifies a set of mental functions that make the transition to thoughts from ideas

---

4 "Philosophy," he says, "does nothing else but transform ideas into thoughts, – and indeed goes further by transforming thoughts into concepts." *G.W.F. Hegel: The Encyclopaedia Logic*, Remark to §20, 50.

possible. These he introduces as diverse forms of memory right after he talks about signs and language.[5]

For Hegel, memory is quite distinct from recollection. Recollection involves bringing back an earlier image on the stimulus of a new intuition. Memory retains words as signs for meanings. It works not with specific individual pictures or experiences, but with meanings – with what is common to all the different *oaks*, all the different ways of *walking*, all the different *clubs* or *associations*. Each one of us may associate these generals with particular mental images, but arbitrary signs now represent them more effectively. It is these signs and their meanings that are central to the role of memory, not our retained images.

The first work of memory is to strengthen the link between a particular meaning and its identifying word and weaken its association with the original sensation or image. It does so in two stages. First, through *retentive memory* we continually reconnect a word with its meaning so that it comes to represent the idea as easily as an image or recalled sensation has done. Language is no longer simply an added decoration, convenient for communication, but becomes central to our use of ideas, even within our own minds.

Then, second, *reproductive memory* finds that it can reproduce and represent the meaning simply by using the word, without recourse to image or impression at all; the meaning immediately brings to mind the word, allowing the image to retreat into the background; and the word directly evokes the meaning. Through constant usage, this becomes second nature, word and sense become inextricably intertwined. A word recalls the sense of some original resemblance; and when we begin to anticipate a sense, we search for the word that signifies it. Whether or not our minds entertain imagined recollections of past experience, we can follow a train of thought as it moves from meaning to meaning.

This close interplay between word and sense has its impact on our use of ideas. As we saw above, we learn a common language by recognizing not so much similarities, but rather the differences that distinguish various meanings. As we internalize our use of words through memory, our ideas become more distinguishable and unique, and we no longer need to focus on retained images. The sign carries with it

5 See G.W.F. Hegel, *Philosophy of Mind*, §§461–4, 219–23.

all the differentiations we have crystallized through our use of language and does so more effectively than an ambiguous mental picture, for it uniquely identifies the delimited resemblance or generality involved. Word and sense become ever more closely intertwined, weaning us from reliance on images recalled from past experience and habituating us to working with the pure resemblance or meaning that words signify.

Hegel, however, adds another step to his account of memory. He talks about our use of *mechanical memory*. The adjective suggests actions that function like machines – automatic, involuntary, lacking originality. He is using the common name for what happens when we learn things by heart without having to think about what we are saying – where words come out without requiring the focus of attention at all.

When we can recite a poem so well that we no longer think of what the words mean, when we routinely say prayers or conventional formulae, when we learn by rote the numbers from one to ten or the names of the players on our favourite football team, we have been developing our mechanical memory. Words now stand on their own. Meanings have disappeared from view. The synthetic connection between meaning and sign that emerges through reproductive memory has collapsed into a simple unity.

Rote learning has a bad press. Educators have abandoned it and instead encourage children to develop their creative imagination. But Hegel, who had been a secondary school headmaster for eight years, adopts a different perspective. A word or name, he says, is a much higher form of mental entity than an image. For the intellect has created words as a way of making our ideas public. So it is "supremely marvellous" that our minds, free and self-contained as they are, can behave in such a mechanical way.[6]

Language is an intellectual creation. Cultures adopt signs to discriminate among meanings and refine them by use over generations. Even though we, as individuals, start out by linking the signs we learn

6 These sentences are from Hegel's lectures of 1827–28: G.W.F. Hegel, *Vorlesungen über die Philosophie des Geistes: Berlin 1827/28*, transcribed by J.E. Erdmann and F. Walter, ed. F. Hespe, B. Tuschlin, et al. (Hamburg: Meiner, 1994), 220–3; English trans. R.R. Williams, *Hegel: Lectures on the Philosophy of Spirit: 1827–28* (Oxford: Oxford University Press, 2007), 233–5.

with meanings drawn from past experience, none the less the words
we use carry the distilled import of cultural history. This basic core is
all that remains when we exercise our mechanical memories. For we
there jettison the encumbrance of our personal associations and allow the words to function simply on their own. They now exist as an
external expression of the work of the human intellect over the years.
While they have lost any sense of relevance to our subjective existence, they retain their role as signs.

The earlier, retentive forms of memory freed the workings of the
mind from reliance on our early impressions and intuitions, as well as
on the retained images or ideas that are the routine cargo of our
minds. Mechanical memory takes us one step further; we now no
longer refer the sign to some personal meaning and back again.
Language functions on its own. But this apparent loss is also a gain.
For the bare words are isolated and dissociated from our personal
history. They are simply audible public forms – the residue of whatever content intellects built into them while interacting over the
course of our culture's development.

This sets the stage for Hegel's critical move. For it is just the mind-
lessness of mechanical memory that makes possible the activity of
thinking, pure and simple. Unfortunately, his explanation of this
shift offers little detail. He says that, because mechanical memory has
dissolved the meanings into the words, there is now no separate, subjective meaning, and our minds are free to focus on the words themselves.[7] We need to explore that distilled comment.

To capture this shift in focus we need move from talk about "meaning" to the language of "significance." I have been using "meaning"
for the personal associations and references of a single mind. In contrast, "significance" points to the sense that words need to have if they
are to be effective instruments of communication. It has a role to play
that is independent of any particular individual.

Words, as I have said above, are creations of intellect; they acquire
their import through the interaction of many minds in conversation.
We originally adopt them as a way of organizing ideas and images,
and to this point in our analysis they have retained that strong connection with our personal histories. But in mechanical memory,

7 Hegel, *Philosophy of Mind*, §464, 223. I work directly with the German text.

the subjectivity of meanings disappears; even the sing-song tone of children that lacks any accent or emphasis captures the emptiness of the words they are speaking. What remains is words – products of the intellect – existing objectively in our speech, but lacking any personal interest or relevance. Mechanical memory has cut them loose from the psychological processes through which they came into being. But, having surrendered our personal interest in these words, we can turn back to them and make them once again the focus of our attention. For the first time, we are free to consider nothing more than what they inherently signify. Abandoning our experience of how the words developed or what they have meant in our past, we bring a dispassionate impartiality to our reflection as we work through the elements of their significance.

Indeed, we can go one step further. Recognizing the way particular perspectives bias our understanding, we are able to counteract their influence. Mechanical memory has exposed the sharp contrast between an interested and a disinterested use of words. Now that our minds can impartially reflect on that use, they can deliberately discount the way our immediate concerns colour ideas and identify those features that are fundamental to communal discourse. Subjective though they be, our minds acquire the capacity to focus simply on the objective content of the words we use.

This is the "supremely marvellous" achievement of mechanical memory. For it has enabled us to rise above the limitations of our personal experience and concentrate simply on the significance of words. It has opened up the possibility of following through implications, no matter where they lead, of examining limitations as well as strengths. Instead of the play of consciousness with its ideas and associations, we have arrived at the disciplined activity of what Kant called "pure reason."

So when we think, we turn our minds to the words we use to discern their significance in a disinterested way. Since these words have now lost all personal meaning and become independent of our psychic histories, we reflect on them as having a life of their own within our culture and society; we explore how people use them and their legitimate connections to each other in intelligible constructions. Even if an image still hangs around, it has lost its crucial status as the place-holder or referent for our intellectual operations. We are free to refine our thoughts, simply by thinking about what they involve.

On this reading, mechanical memory has broken the rigid connection between word and personal meaning and allows sense and significance to acquire an objective and independent character. Our minds explore abstractions that require no phenomenal embodiment in our imagination. It is too early to start talking about the full objectivity of Frege's concepts. But these pure thoughts, divorced from both originating image and associated idea, have introduced a psychological activity of a new and different order – a world, like that of Galton's scientists, where subjectivity has a much-reduced role to play.

Thus memory – both retentive and mechanical – makes possible a transition from ideas to thoughts, establishing a bridge over which our minds are free to move. We are no longer dependent on the causal necessity of unconscious association or the arbitrary constructs of our imagination. We can reflect on and modify our thoughts, exploring how they function. This achievement opens the way for Hegel's second transformation: from thoughts to concepts.

6

Thoughts and Descartes's Rules

IF HEGEL'S SUGGESTION IS CORRECT, memory can wean our minds from the influence of personal interests and limited perspectives. We no longer need retained images and recollections to represent our meanings, for, through reproductive memory, words perform the task more effectively and precisely. Mechanical memory goes further; for it abandons personal meaning itself and lets words simply function on their own. The mind is free to focus on them in a disinterested way. It pays attention to the import that they have acquired in our culture over the years. To be sure, we have made our own small contribution to that retained significance, but the way the terms function more widely in the universe of discourse takes pride of place. As we become aware of our subjective prejudices and biases, we discount their value and look beyond them for a more objective perspective. We consider pure thoughts: the public significance of the words we use. We are coming close to whatever operations of the intellect enable us to grasp, or think through, concepts.

But we need to be careful as we proceed. For pure thoughts start out being quite vague and indistinct. To be sure, they contain the discriminations we learned as we acquired our vocabulary; but these retain the contingencies and ambiguities of all social interaction. Words function differently in different contexts; so variation and imprecision muddy whatever significance they carry. In public discourse, every participant brings a limited perspective to her or his use of language. Through the use of metaphor and subtle misunderstandings, words change their sense; they take on usages that would have been unintelligible to an earlier generation. That lack of clarity confronts us once thoughts become the primary focus of our attention. It is hard to have a clear sense of their significance. This is why many of us fall back on familiar images that represent repeated features of our experience. They have the aura of being concrete and specific. Although they may be ambiguous in their reference, they have a definite character.

Vagueness, however, cries out for precision. In acquiring a public language, we have already developed skills in refining words so that they discriminate among a variety of meanings. We have learned how misunderstandings arise and taken steps to avoid them. So we already have to hand mental operations that we can adapt to this more abstract context.

In the narrative so far – as we moved from intuition, through recollection, the formation of ideas and imagination, to words and memory – the mind is active in various ways. Attention *focuses* on particular moments within the panorama of our immediate experience; what it notices is *stored* in our subconscious; recollection *draws on* resemblances that link some new intuition to images retained there; imagination *brings moments together* into a synthesis, drawing not only on resemblances, but on context, both recalled and newly generated; we *acquire* a common language by becoming aware of distinctions and differences among closely related ideas; memory not only *melds* word and meaning so closely together that they become a simple unity, but also enables words with their implicit import to *function* on their own. These operations are not dependent on the particular content provided by our sensible intuition and the imaginative products of recollection. They are plastic enough to operate on other material as well, such as those pure thoughts that are now the focus of our concern.

So our intellects can focus on the thoughts behind the words, noticing how some resemble each other and how they are none the less distinguishable. They can bring words together into synthetic combinations and even integrate them so effectively that we require new words to signify the complex networks of thought that result. No longer functioning as ways we come to terms with personal experience, these operations can serve to clarify our thinking and contribute to the more effective functioning of public discourse.

The new context, however, affects the way words perform their tasks. To provide some guidance in exploring how thought appropriates these intellectual skills for its own purposes, it is useful to turn once again to the tradition – this time to the rationalism of René

Descartes. In the same century that Locke and his successors tried to resolve the dilemma of conflicting claims to truth through an appeal to immediate sensation, Descartes sought a firm foundation within the realm of pure thought – in what he called "clear and distinct ideas."[1]

In his *Principles of Philosophy* (I, 45), Descartes defines these two characteristics: "I call 'clear' a cognition that is present and evident to the attentive mind; 'distinct,' one which is so precise and differentiated from everything else that it contains only what appears clearly to the one who considers it in an appropriate manner."[2] Here we find several terms that pick up on our earlier discussion. Clarity comes from *attention* ("the attentive mind"), the same kind of attention we pay whenever we want to identify what is going on in our minds. Distinctness, in contrast, comes from *differentiating* our thought from any others that might contaminate it – drawing boundaries that define its limits, focusing on what is essential; this process is a more rigorous and self-conscious form of the one we use as we develop language skills. Descartes elaborates on the role of these operations in his *Discourse on Method*, where he outlines four rules that disciplined thinking should follow. These will provide us with a framework for our investigation into the way thinking operates.

His *first rule* introduces us to the realm of thought: "never to accept anything as true if I did not have evident knowledge of its truth: that is, carefully to avoid precipitate conclusions and preconceptions, and to include nothing more in my judgements than what presented itself to my mind so clearly and so distinctly that I had no occasion to doubt it."[3]

Descartes was searching for absolute certainty, free from all doubt. Our quest is more modest. We are not in a position where we can easily claim that there are thoughts we cannot doubt, even when they are clear and distinct. We have identified thoughts with words that have become the common currency of our culture, and those words, for all their objective independence from our personal interests, are

1 Once again, we encounter the ambiguity of the term "idea." In the language that Frege and his translators use, Descartes is talking about concepts.

2 The passage appears in *The Philosophical Works of Descartes*, trans. J. Cottingham, R. Stoothoff, and D. Murdoch (Cambridge: Cambridge University Press, 1985), Vol. I, 207–8. I provide my own translation, since Cottingham et al. use "perception" for "*connaisance*," which makes Descartes sound much more empiricist than he really is.

3 *Discourse on Method*, Part 2, in *Philosophical Works*, I, 120.

affected by a variety of perspectives and uses. To decide on their ultimate significance, we need to work out carefully how we should use
them. But this clarity and precision will not, on its own, result in
truth. So what is important in this rule, for our purposes, is not the
goal it intends to achieve, but the procedure it recommends: "to
avoid precipitate conclusions and preconceptions, and to include
nothing more in my judgements than what presented itself to my
mind ... clearly and ... distinctly."

Clarity and distinctness can belong to only those thoughts that,
through the medium of memory, we have liberated from the peculiarities of our idiosyncratic experience and that have begun to function on their own. As we saw above, this requires our avoiding hasty
conclusions and discounting biases and personal prejudices. In other
words, this first rule identifies the initial step thinking takes, when it
looks at the results of mechanical memory and considers words on
their own in a disinterested way.

Descartes's conviction that we can proceed effectively only when
we know exactly what we are thinking is worth taking seriously. We
need to take care that we focus our mind not on ideas we casually
recall from past experience, but on thoughts. By eliminating vagueness from these, we can guard against precipitate judgments that
could lead us astray. In other words, we now turn the act of paying
attention, which first surfaces in intuition when we concentrate on
only some of the things our senses present to us and which plays a
role throughout the development of ideas, towards the products of
the community of discourse. By centring its interest on pure thoughts,
our minds abstract from contingent associations deriving from particular experiences and reflect simply on the sense that words signify.
Such a move is the first step in dispelling the vagueness that clouds
our thinking.

Descartes's *second rule* picks up the theme of differentiation: "to
divide each of the difficulties I examined into as many parts as possible and as may be required in order to resolve them better." Although
we are working not primarily to resolve difficulties, we do want to
clarify our thoughts. In performing this task, we should seek to divide
their sense into as many components as possible so that we can resolve their imprecision and identify their essential characteristics.
Once we have dispassionately focused on our thoughts, we need to
dissect them to see what their use and significance involve. Here we

draw on the discriminations we learned as we developed our vocabulary. We have noticed that some words share a similar sense, yet have specific differences, all of which contribute in various ways to its significance. The similarities and the differences become separate and distinct thoughts. This capacity to discriminate, which we already noticed in our acquisition of a language, becomes more rigorous as it concentrates on the products of pure thought. It works simply with the sense of the term and ignores whatever might come from our peculiar psychological history. This activity of division and analysis deserves a chapter on its own, to which we turn in chapter 7.

Descartes's *third rule* deals with synthesis. Being able to break up something into its components is useful only if we can then put them back together. If we are going to be successful in thinking thoughts, we must have some strategy for combining them into more complex ones. So the work of analysis provides only half of the picture. Just as imagination is able to take various representations and consider them together in a synthesis, whether immediately in a stream of consciousness or deliberately through creative fantasy, so in the realm of pure thought the intellect needs to assemble various distinct senses into more developed and sophisticated constructions. In his third rule, accordingly, Descartes suggests that a rational method requires such a skill: "to direct my thoughts in an orderly manner, by beginning with the simplest and most easily known objects in order to ascend little by little, step by step, to the knowledge of the most complex, and by supposing some order even among objects that have no natural order of precedence."

Unfortunately, that rule tells us little about the way we are to use our minds to "ascend" this hierarchy. How are we to link simple notions together into more complex thoughts? That requires order, which suggests that there must be some kind of justification for the connections. But we can no longer rely on the strategies of imagination. Subconscious associations, the free syntheses of fantasy, and even the adoption of arbitrary signs are all the work of a mind embedded in the realm of ideas. Having put that world behind us, and isolated words through the discriminating capacity of our thought, we are left with simple terms that appear to have no immediate relation to each other. All we can derive from Descartes's third rule is the need for some kind of synthesis – one that, while bringing various thoughts together, does not leave them in a jumble but produces something that can become clear and distinct. But Descartes does not define the specific nature of that operation. We explore the act of synthesis in chapter 8.

But Descartes does not stop there. He introduces a *fourth rule*: "throughout to make enumerations so complete, and reviews so comprehensive, that I could be sure of leaving nothing out." Here he suggests that limiting ourselves to the strategies of analysis and synthesis is not enough. We have to go beyond the limits of the thoughts already in our minds and look for a wider context. Our reviews must be "comprehensive"; we must look for all those details and aspects that have some kind of influence on the questions we are considering. Our "enumerations" must be "complete"; we must check the whole realm of our thoughts to see that we have omitted nothing. Such a rule presents new challenges. Now we have to turn back to our subconscious and deliberately recall from that "dark pit" whatever might conceivably have some relevance to our project. No longer are we instinctively recollecting images and experiences. We are rather trying to pull out all the elements of sense that have embedded themselves in our minds as, over time, we have appropriated the wisdom of our culture. So this kind of recollection is not a return to the images that we have attached to our ideas within our personal experience; it is rather an investigation of words and thoughts that have disappeared from our current considerations into the reservoir of our subconscious memory.

Even this, however, is not enough. For such reflection can deal with only the words that happened to emerge in our interaction with the social world around us. Since, in the past, there have been times when we entered into an unknown discipline and encountered a rich treasury of terms that expose a wide range of significant thoughts not previously known, we would be presumptuous to assume that there is nothing more for us to learn – that our present vocabulary, active and potential, is fully comprehensive. Indeed, the history of science and of human exploration recounts times when a whole culture has suddenly discovered realms of significance that triggered a revolution in its thinking. This means that we cannot satisfy Descartes's fourth rule by drawing simply on what our own culture's vocabulary has retained.

To even approach the goal of comprehensiveness, we need to find ways of investigating distinct characteristics of the world itself – the world that exists beyond our limited experience, and indeed the limited experience of the human species. Somehow we must move beyond our idiosyncratic histories to discover features of the universe relevant to our quest for comprehensive thoughts, and essential if we are to achieve some suggestion of completeness. Descartes seems to assume that, by reviewing what we already have within our minds and enumerating everything contained there, we can satisfy the requirement of comprehensiveness. But disciplined thinking is required if we are to challenge the biased perspective of even this supposedly impartial program. Comprehensiveness presents a greater challenge than Descartes had assumed. So we return in chapter 9 to this final requirement.

Thus Descartes has given us four rules to follow as our minds reflect on their thoughts. There is *limiting our attention* to the realm of thoughts themselves; there is *analysis*: the separation of distinct and discrete parts or moments; there is *synthesis*: the ability to organize a collection of such thoughts into more complex wholes; and there is *comprehensiveness*: considering the whole context within which we are thinking to ensure that we have as adequate a thought as we can produce. The first of these emerged already as implicit in the transition from mechanical memory to thinking. The other three, however, are general and programmatic. We need to examine each in more detail so we can see how to refine our thoughts to the point where we are able to grasp Frege's concepts. What kinds of analysis are most successful? How can we produce a synthesis that satisfies our need for precise thoughts? And what do we do, when investigating the whole realm of our intellectual activity, to ensure that the characteristics we discern not only satisfy our need for clarity, but also do justice to the world in which we live? If we are to proceed further in our quest, we need to identify more precisely what each of these three operations contributes to crystallizing our thoughts.

7

Second Rule: Analysis and Definition

TO MOVE OUR THOUGHTS AWAY from vague ambiguity to some measure of precision, we need to identify their core significance. This involves focusing on each one and distinguishing within it those features that are distinctive, while setting aside related aspects that are not relevant. In other words, we follow Descartes's second rule: "to divide each of the difficulties I examined into as many parts as possible and as may be required in order to resolve them better."

But what are the "parts" of a thought? A sense or meaning is not like a watch or car, where we can take it apart, piece by piece, in order to see how it is put together. It seems more like an amorphous blob that has indistinct edges and simply flows as a vague continuum. Yet it is possible to analyse even blobs: look for the kind of thing they are; figure out how they differ from similar substances; and notice how they interact with their immediate environment.

We can make similar moves with our thoughts. A first move involves clarifying their general context by gradually restricting its range. We might start, for example, with the thought of being short of money. Since that can cover a variety of circumstances, we narrow in on one: we do not mean just lacking cash in one's pocket when making a purchase, but rather not having the resources generally to do what we want to do. Then, we limit it further to the finances of a business operation. Within that context, we could focus on a single year when it spent more money that it took in, or on a sequence of years in which expenditures exceeded income. In this way, we narrow down the original generality to the distinction between deficit and debt. And we are then able to decide which meaning is the one relevant to our immediate interests, for example, "deficit."

The initial thought of being short of money is rather like the basic makeup of our blob. We have been able to approach the nucleus of our thought by establishing limits that separate it from other possible senses. Since our goal is a clear sense of what we are thinking about, the process could go further. Economists, for example, differentiate a structural deficit, a function of the way the business operates, from one that is the result of contingent factors not likely to recur.

In the course of this analysis, we have divided our amorphous thought into a number of distinct parts, some of which we have been able to set aside. And this has enabled us to render it more distinct.

We have been describing what happens when we define terms. And it happens strictly within the domain of thought. Any reference to ideas would confuse the issue. It does not help to recall the time we overdrew the bank account, to imagine a balance sheet, or to appeal to Mr Micawber's comment: "Income twenty shillings; expenditure twenty shillings one pence; result misery. Income twenty shillings; expenditure nineteen shillings eleven pence; result happiness."[1] Past experiences and illustrative examples present two difficulties. First, they are rich and complex events, which can be interpreted in a number of ways. Since they embody a number of possible relations, we can eliminate ambiguity only by appealing to impartial thought to focus on the aspects that are relevant and exclude those that are not. Second, the ideas through which we recall these experiences exercise no control over the generalities they represent. They emerge from the subconscious in contingent and haphazard ways. They do not tell us which, of the many references an image represents, may be significant. And the only clues they can provide to inform us how they link with other ideas are chance associations, emerging again from the subconscious, or the products of creative imagination. When people try to define terms by pointing to an instance – what philosophers call "ostensive definitions" – the result is frequently unsatisfactory, because people direct their attention in different directions or focus on different aspects. The ideas they appeal to need not be the same. An ostensive definition is successful only when it presupposes thoughtful analysis. Ideas do not help to clarify a term. We cannot escape using reflection and thought.

1 Charles Dickens, *Great Expectations.* At the time, twelve pence equalled a shilling.

Another strategy for clarifying our terms is an appeal to synonyms – other words that have a similar sense and can be used in similar situations. But that does not take us very far, either. For we have simply pushed the question back one step: we now require some clear analysis of the synonym. If that is not available, we are simply using two different words or signs for a single, indefinite sense, and we are no further ahead. Even where we already know the synonym, we may require more: subtle distinctions that discriminate between appropriate uses of the two terms. We need analysis and differentiation.

In other words, analysis identifies various elements critical to the sense of the word in question. And the most effective form of definition, Aristotle notes, starts from a general sense, and draws distinctions within it: "The framer of a definition," he writes in the *Topics*, "should first place the object in its genus, and then append its differences."[2] There is a kind of hierarchy. From the most general, we descend, drawing more and more precise differentiations, until we have given the thought its distinctive form. We separate the term's "genus" from a range of "differences."

We start by distinguishing the genus. This is already implicit in our thoughts. Linguistic signs signify something common that a number of immediate impressions and ideas share. They already contain a generality. And the more general of these acquire currency in our thoughts and conversations as we learn to use a common language with some measure of competence. For all that those meanings may be vague, they none the less have a distinctive character. And that provides a basis from which we can proceed to clarify our thoughts. Despite its vagueness and breadth, this general sense will continue to be a significant constituent in the final characterization of our term. This enables us to isolate one appropriate general context from the range of thoughts that clutter our mind.

Then we introduce differences. A general term includes a number of options and possibilities. We need to exclude some in a gradual process, reducing step by step the range of application. Each act of exclusion sets a limit, beyond which this particular thought does not

---

2 *Topics*, VI, i, 139ª27, from *The Complete Works of Aristotle*, ed. J. Barnes, Bollingen Series (Princeton, NJ: Princeton University Press, 1984), LXXI, Vol. 1, 235. Again, in the *Metaphysics*, he writes: "The definition is the formula which contains the differentiae, or, according to the right method, the last of these" *Metaphysics* Z (VII), xii, 1038ª28–30, from ibid., V, Vol. II, 1639.

apply. At the same time, it makes more definite just what we are thinking about. Aristotle suggests that there is only one significant difference in any definition. But there may in fact be many. Meanings do
not fall easily into a single hierarchy. Relations stretch out in many
different directions; so we need to restrict and reject possible alternatives in a variety of ways.

The definition of "give," for example, as "make another the recipient of something in a subject's possession"[3] starts from the generic
sense of some action, "make," but then limits it to situations where
there is not only an agent but also a recipient, and an object transferred, initially the property of the subject. We have here a very complex set of differentiae. Two agents participate in the action, neither
one nor three. An object passes from one to the other; the interaction is no simple social conversation, nor is it a physical struggle for
dominance. The object starts out belonging to the subject and ends
up in the hands of the recipient; the two are not playing a game like
badminton with reciprocal exchanges, nor are they taking turns at
splitting a log of hard maple by handing an axe back and forth. And
the transfer happens at the initiative of the subject; the recipient does
not steal or wrench the object from her.

These differentiae not only identify this particular definition, but
also exclude related possibilities. They come into play at various levels, gradually distinguishing how this limited term fits into its broader
context of intentional action. In a similar way, any definition contains
a number of constituents, to each of which we give a precise sense by
excluding related meanings.

Defining thus involves a double action: one *affirms* a particular feature by *excluding* others that are implicit in the genus. We identify
positive content by using negatives. The latter are as much a part of
the definition as the former, for they establish the limits beyond
which the sense does not apply. By saying what something is not, we
approach a sense of what it is. And these negatives remain as implicit
elements of its meaning.

Whenever we define our thoughts, we adopt this kind of analysis –
identifying differences within a genus. And that double process –
generalizing and differentiating– happens as a process of thought,
not of ideas. Ideas, with their images and representations, remain

3 This is the general sense in *Oxford Concise Dictionary*, 4th ed. (1951), 508.

ambiguous and vague until we have submitted them to careful reflection – a reflection that requires that we draw distinctions. Yet there is
no image of "not" that can be the basis of an idea.[4] The act of comparison, by which we differentiate, involves the initiative of our intellects – a conscious decision that introduces a precision that would
not otherwise be there.

This process of definition is rather like the process we use to discriminate among meanings as we appropriate a common language.
In both, we start out thinking that some general term will suffice, and
in both we learn to distinguish several distinct meanings as we find
our efforts lead to misunderstanding and confusion. The interplay of
similarity and difference that structures mutual recognition finds its
counterpart in the relationship our thinking draws between genus
and specific difference.

---

4 Gregory Bateson writes in his Metalogue "What Is an Instinct?" in Bateson, *Steps
to an Ecology of Mind* (Northvale, NJ: Jason Aronson, 1987), 54–5:
   D. ... Is there any 'not' in animal behavior?
   F. How could there be?
   D. I mean can an animal say by its actions, ... 'I am not biting you'?
   F. ... If the animal *is* not biting the other, he's not biting it, and that's it.
   D. But he might not be doing all sorts of other things, sleeping, eating, running,
and so on. How can he say, 'It's biting I'm not doing'?
   F. He can only do that if biting has somehow been mentioned.
   D. Do you mean that he could say, 'I am not biting you' by first showing his
fangs and *then* not biting?
   F. Yes. Something like that.
   D. But what about *two* animals? They'd both have to show their fangs.
   F. Yes.
   D. And, it seems to me, they might misunderstand each other and get into
a fight.
   F. Yes. There is always that danger when you deal in opposites and do not or
cannot say what you are doing, especially when you do not *know* what you are
doing.
   D. But the animals would know that they bared their fangs in order to say, 'I
won't bite you.'
   F. I doubt whether they would know. Certainly neither animal knows it about
the other ...
   D. Then it's a sort of experiment ...
   F. Yes.
   D. So they might get into a fight in order to find out whether fighting was what
they had to do.
   F. Yes – but I'd rather put it less purposively – that the fight shows them what
sort of relationship they have, after it. It's not planned.
   D. Then 'not' is really not there when the animals show their fangs.

There is, however, a difference. We learn a public language through use, noticing where a term or phrase functions appropriately and where they fail. We respond to the reactions of our fellows. But what we learn from this can often result in vague and improper practice. I grew up, for example, thinking that "inimitable" meant something like "delightfully attractive"; and I was quite shocked to discover that others meant "that which defies imitation." For all that I was able to use the term reasonably effectively in the contexts in which I lived, I was nevertheless communicating something I never intended. In a similar way, much of the common currency of daily speech remains vague and imprecise. The social dynamic of mutual recognition cannot ensure accurate thoughts.

When we define through analysis, however, the act of discrimination is deliberate. We start out with vagueness and ambiguity, then draw distinctions, demarcating a boundary between the sense being defined and others that initially seem related. We focus not only on the various alternatives, but on how and why they differ from each other. And, if someone challenges us, we can provide reasons for the decisions we have made. Usually, we are ready to adopt the conventions of our culture, as we find them in one or another dictionary. At times, however, we find they too can be imprecise, as words shift in meaning over time and from one region to another. So we stipulate which particular sense we have in mind and restrict our use of terms to fit that definition. It is in this way that we articulate the specific thoughts we have in mind.

There is, however, another way by which the words of our language do not map directly onto the thoughts we define, for words and thoughts are not isomorphic.

Each word is a unit, separate from its associates. In speech, one word may very well elide into another, and in some languages a speaker can·inflect a term to indicate how it is to relate to other elements of a sentence, but it serves as a tool of communication only because we can isolate it from its context and use it elsewhere, in other settings. Particularly in languages such as English, where there is little inflection of roots to indicate tense or mood of verbs, case or gender of nouns and adjectives, we come to think that each word is a unit with no intrinsic relation to any others; only when we combine them in order to communicate do the resulting molecules acquire a broader meaning. It is not surprising, then, that we extend this understanding to the thoughts that words signify and think of each as an independent, atomic unit that has no intrinsic link to any others.

Transferring the independence of individual words to the thoughts they express is, however, misleading. When, in the process of definition, we set limits for the terms we are thinking, the result retains implicit traces of the path by which we reached it. And its core sense includes a range of what I am going to call "tendrils" that reach out to other senses in both positive and negative ways. Our thought of "deficit" has links with the thoughts of being short of money, of being a business or other operation with organized accounts, of being distinct from having debts, and of being either structural or contingent. These links reach up to the genus, across barriers to the senses left behind, and down to subsidiary species. In other words, thoughts are not as independent and isolated as our use of words would suggest. When we analyse them to formulate definitions, the result incorporates and retains all the subordinations and differentiations we introduced along the way.[5] As we see below in part II, these tendrils, inherent in the meanings of the terms we have defined, play a significant role in our thinking.

Let us first consider the relation between genus and species. We have identified the general because it is plastic and can incorporate a number of different sorts of specification within it. Its determinate meaning includes all those implicit and potential relationships. Indeed it is just this range of multiple implications that requires the introduction of the differentiae. "Colour," for example, implies that one can flesh it out with a wide range of shades. At the same time, those differences presuppose and rely on the genus within which they function. The thought of "purple" has links with "colour"; "colour" is a specific kind of "quality" that tends to characterize some "surface." These connections are not simply the result of associations among ideas, as when our minds move from the colour "purple" to imperial courts, to elaborate and colourful prose, or to pretension or

---

5 In our mechanistically minded world, we assume that the end result of analysis is a set of independent units, each in isolation from the others, and which we need only collect together to reconstruct our original term. But the object with which we began is itself an integrated whole, which means that each one of the parts has some kind of link with the others. If, at the end of our analysis, we cannot explain how the parts fit together, we have failed in our task.

pomposity. They are rather part of the meaning of the terms we have defined; they emerge from deliberate and conscious reflection on the hierarchies central to any decent definition. Though not explicit in the words we use, these intrinsic relationships or tendrils are none the less essential to the thoughts we signify. In our disciplined formulation of definitions, there are implicit connections that can lead our thoughts up and down a scale – to related terms that are both more general and more specific.

A similar network of relationships develops from the use of differentiae to exclude. The deliberate use of negation is quite different from the act of differentiating among various ideas as we appropriate the signs of a shared language. In the act of definition, the particle "not" has several distinct meanings. On rare occasions, we may use it to mean that the subject "has nothing at all to do with" the predicate; it distinguishes something from its contradictory. Usually, however, we imply that the item we want to identify, and the one we are excluding, both function within the same general context: they are alternate species within a single genus; exclusive contraries within a framework they none the less share. So, whenever we draw distinctions to refine our definition, we implicitly point to a framework of meaning where the contrasting features play a critical role. In the context of this study, for example, a thought is *not* an idea or an image. The specific meaning of our defined term includes the fact that we exclude these, its relatives. And that exclusion is an important part of its central significance.

If we return to our earlier instance of "give," we can provide an example of how this extension works. At that time, we said: "An object is introduced that passes from one to the other; the interaction is no simple social conversation, nor is it a physical struggle for dominance. The object starts out belonging to the subject and ends up in the hands of the recipient; the two are not playing a game like badminton with reciprocal exchanges, nor are they taking turns at splitting a log of hard maple by handing an axe back and forth." Anthropological theory has looked at this primary definition of gifts and begun to question it by asking whether it in fact excludes all these alternatives. In societies where giving gifts has become a major social phenomenon, they say, it turns into its opposite: each recipient feels the obligation to provide a gift in return, making it a moment of reciprocal exchange. In others, chiefs or leaders can, by expanding the largesse of their donations, demonstrate their dominance as if they were playing a competitive game. It was the implicit exclusions in the original meaning, which thought identified, that led to the questioning of their appropriateness. Reflective theory found a significant link implicit in an exclusive "not." It uncovered tendrils that relate one thought to differentiated others.

Thus defined thoughts have tendrils that reach out upwards to their more general contexts, sideways to the alternatives that their differentiae exclude, and downwards to the species they include. Because these tendrils are characteristics of thoughts, not of the words people use to express them, it is tempting to think that they are subjective and personal – that they do not apply to the objective world of meanings which develops through social discourse. But this fails to notice how in that discourse we continually rely on the whole structure of implicit connections. We have been able to communicate with our fellows because they too understand the relation between general terms and the particulars that we differentiate within them; they too have refined their thoughts by understanding the implications of the particle "not." The tendrils that subdivide generals into particulars, and exclude particulars from each other, have become part of that whole network of significance. Within the public realm of intelligent discourse, they have benefited from the focus of thoughtful reflection.

The implicit links we have identified – the tendrils that reach out from a thought to others closely related – are an important feature of even the most precisely defined term. Indeed, they are plastic enough to expand. We may notice that there are other connecting links beyond those that stem from our definitions. We may discover the need to introduce new contrasts into our public discussions. We may find links to other thoughts that serve as complements or enhancements. The discourse within which a community defines and refines its vocabulary constantly adjusts the senses, even when strictly delimiting them. The realm of pure thoughts is never static.

We can now bring this discussion to a close. We have identified two different aspects in the analysis or definition of a thought: one that identifies the hierarchy of genus and species within which the particular meaning is to fit; another that excludes related senses that also operate within that hierarchy. This twofold process can be the work of a single mind, reflecting on its thoughts and refining them to articulate its meaning precisely. But it can also be a feature of public discourse – that realm of intersubjective and public meaning that outlasts any one individual's attention span or mental existence. More than this, we have found that this realm of public meaning contains within it, hiding behind the atomism of our written and spoken vocabulary, implicit tendrils that reach out and connect elements of meaning to one another, either as correlatives mutually related or as contraries explicitly excluded. Through analysis, the realm of thought is able to move beyond the idiosyncratic realm of subjective ideas, tied to our individual experiences, into a more public arena.

By introducing our discussion of implicit tendrils of meaning, we have raised, however, a second concern. For thoughts frequently use these links to integrate a complex of meanings into a single conception or notion. This is a process of synthesis, not of analysis. In the next chapter, we turn to examine this second kind of reflective operation.

8

Third Rule: Synthesis and Unity

THROUGH ANALYSIS, we identify the components of individual thoughts – various levels of genera and a range of specific differences. Thoughts, however, can also be complex, integrating a large number of disparate elements. If we want to understand what the phrase "exchange rate" involves, for example, we start by focusing on the relationship of national currencies to each other. But when we explore further, we find that this thought relates to more far-reaching aspects of our political economy: the monetary policy of central banks, government fiscal policy, international trade, the efficiency of the manufacturing sector, the ease of developing natural resources such as wood, minerals, and petroleum. Somehow, all of these are linked together within the confines of a single thought. Careful reflection, then, involves connecting meanings to each other as much as taking them apart – synthesis as well as analysis, construction as well as definition.

In our earlier scenario in chapter 3 of how ideas develop, imagination is the agent of synthesis. Initially, it associates one idea with another in our stream of consciousness, at times with a regularity that Sherlock Holmes could exploit to confound Dr Watson, breaking into his thoughts with an apposite comment. But such associations are derived from the way our experiences happen to follow one another in time and from our particular spatial perspective. They do not have the rigid, lawlike pattern that nineteenth-century empiricist psychologists assumed.

In a second function, imagination links idea to idea through metaphor or fantasy. Here, however, its syntheses are spontaneous and reflect our individual interests and predilections. There is nothing controlling these creative actions to ensure that they capture anything more than our personal, and subjective, intentions.

The question that now arises is whether there is any means by which pure thought can move beyond the contingencies of the imagination and create syntheses that apply outside the limited perspective of personal experience. Is there a way of linking thought to thought that maintains the clarity and precision of disciplined reflection? Such a move would not simply bring various senses together into an arbitrary collection, but would find ways to integrate them into a coherent unity. The interconnections would follow from the content being thought, not from the predispositions of the thinker. Clear and precise thoughts require more than the simple juxtaposition of metaphor or analogy: the various elements need to mesh together with some measure of inevitability, and each link requires a justification that reaches beyond the peculiarities of personal experience.

Immanuel Kant draws just this distinction between the syntheses of imagination and what he calls the "discursive unities" generated by thought.[1] Imagination creates associations and parallels; it is not limited to what is present to our senses but can incorporate elements from the vast resources of our sub-conscious. Because we can recall experiences imaginatively, we can bring a wide range of ideas within a single perspective. But, as Kant says, "even this does not yield knowledge." It takes place within our subjective consciousness and draws on our personal past history. In a synthesis, we view two components within a single perspective. But even when those components are thoughts, they retain their independence, for all that we notice similarities and differences, recall times when they emerged together in

---

1 In *Critique of Pure Reason*, A789/B104: "What transcendental logic ... teaches is how we bring to concepts, not representations, but the pure synthesis of representations. What must first be given – with a view to the a priori knowledge of all objects – is the manifold of pure intuition; the second factor involved is the synthesis of this manifold by means of the imagination. But even this does not yield knowledge. The concepts which give unity to this pure synthesis, and which consist solely in the representation of this necessary synthetic unity, furnish the third requisite for the knowledge of an object; and they rest on the understanding" (trans. Kemp Smith, London: Macmillan, 1953, 112). For the moment I shall refrain from using the language of conceiving and concepts and rely on Kant's "understanding," because I do not want to introduce terms that would short circuit Frege's demand that concepts be objective and independent of the subjectivity of ideas.

our past, or suggest that the conjunction may be illuminating. Syntheses may be instructive, but their association remains contingent; each item continues separate and self-contained.

Knowledge, however, requires something more. The synthesis, or simple aggregation, needs to become united, and the contingent and arbitrary associations need to be transformed into necessary connections.

This is why Kant contrasts the contingency of imagination with the discursive role of understanding. The thinking of thoughts, unlike the syntheses of imagination, involves what he calls "functions" – acts that integrate various senses and meanings into a single thought. In this way, a synthesis becomes a *unity*. By distinguishing between these two operations, he indicates that, in a unity, the various terms lose their atomic independence and become linked as components of a single thought. The functions of thinking have transformed them into interlocking elements that complement and require each other. They integrate what is simply conjoined. It is as if we have moved from a simple mixture of hydrogen and oxygen in the atmosphere to drops of water, where they so bond to each other that it is no longer easy to separate them. This, says Kant, is the work of understanding, and it produces objective concepts

But this leaves Kant with a problem. Even though our minds are active in creating these unities, and even though we may find ways of integrating various thoughts into "a common representation," the result may still be arbitrary and subjective. Our minds, in thinking, are under few constraints and can easily manufacture connections that draw on personal perspectives and particular interests. If we want to move beyond our restricted subjectivity and generate thoughts that have some objective status – that hold independent of our experience and can be communicated effectively to others – we need something more.

This problem Kant tackles later in his first *Critique* in the "Second Analogy."[2] In this section, his task is to explain how we can distinguish a sequence that is objective and causal from one that is just the temporal order of our subjective experiences. Cause introduces a feature not present in the way sensations and immediate intuitions

2 See *Critique of Pure Reason*, A189–211/B232–56, trans. N. Kemp Smith (New York: Macmillan, 1973), 218–33.

follow one another in time. The events we encounter through our senses offer no reasons for the order in which they happen to appear. So Kant had to show why we draw a distinction between two types of sequence within our experience – one that applies objectively, independent of our subjective stream of consciousness, and another, which reflects nothing more than the peculiarities of our personal history.

Kant's solution to this challenge starts with the fact that "causal" relations happen according to a rule: two events correlate with each other in a regular way. Not only this, but we can find a justification for this regularity. One of the events is not simply the predecessor of the other, but there is a sufficient reason for their order. In other words, one looks for some general structure that explains the relationship. This inherent link, says Kant, justifies our transforming a particular temporal sequence in our subjective experience into the thought of a causal relationship. It enables us to move beyond recollecting a simple "before and after" in our imagination to understanding that a connection holds objectively.

Kant leaves his discussion at this point. But from this analysis, we can draw two implications that are useful for our purposes. First, what is the source of the conditions that are to justify causal judgments? What can constitute "sufficient reasons"? They cannot come from our immediate sensations. Since the spatial and temporal limitations of our subjective experience shape these sensations, they can tell us nothing definitive about the world as it really is. And the particular sensible qualities we experience impinge on our senses as radical givens; according to Kant, we receive them passively. Even if they recur time and again so that they seem to be an example of Hume's "constant conjunction," we need more. We must seek a rule, a principle of thought, that connects them – that requires our thoughts to move from one to another and integrate them into the concept of cause. This rule cannot be directly present in our experiences. Nor can it simply be the result of habit and custom. Some intellectual process needs to intervene, working with the material of our sensible intuitions and transforming them into the currency of reflection.

If experience presents us with evidence so strong that we find in it a sufficient reason for binding one to another, this can come only from our ability to take the givens of sensation as signs of something else – as evidence of what we have been calling a "thought." And these thoughts must not function as atomic and isolated units, but reach out and establish conditioning relations with one another. For the content of experience to move beyond bare qualities and provide evidence for causal connection, the thoughts it generates must provide us with something rather like the tendrils I introduced in the last chapter. As we think about what has happened, a tentative link reaches out from one of them and connects with a receptive feature implicit in the other. These tendrils transform the simple synthesis into a linked interconnection.

But, second, we require something more. Kant has introduced a very strong claim: that the links are sufficiently determinate to exclude all other possible connections. We are, he suggests, able to find "*the* condition under which an event invariably and necessarily follows"; we can in some way become certain that only one subsequent event is in the cards.

A condition is a state or event that makes something else possible. But a single condition need not be sufficient of itself to make that other happen with necessity. To do that it usually has to combine with a set of other conditions that set the stage and influence the outcome. These coalesce at one particular point to bring about the result. Only when we take all of them into account can we say that we have a *sufficient* reason for its emergence; simply lumping them together is not enough. To identify such a set as sufficient, we have to show that there are no other surrounding circumstances that are relevant; and simply appealing to the fact that the effect occurred will not satisfy this demand. Rather, the various components of the set need to be interconnected. Their various tendrils must link together in ways that are consistent among themselves. And this coherence is to be so well integrated that it would seem to be complete. The various thoughts interconnect in a comprehensive and inclusive way. This act of thinking, in which we integrate a complex of thoughts into a single, comprehensive unity, is what Kant calls "understanding."

He has limited the role of sufficient reason to establishing the objectivity of causal connections. But we can extend it much further. Whenever we look for an explanation for why things happen the way they do, we are exploring how a variety of different thoughts can be interconnected into a complex, yet coherent and integrated conception. Explanation, like understanding, involves functions that happen in the realm of thought; they never emerge simply from the imaginative flow of ideas. They build on tendrils implicit in the thoughts that people share and that have been liberated from the relativity of subjective experience.

Kant's argument in the "Second Analogy" helps us resolve our immediate question: how, in thought, we can integrate conjoined syntheses into integrated conceptions. In the process of forming clear and distinct thoughts, the discursive intellect appeals to interconnections and correlations that are not a function of immediate sensations, nor of imaginative ideas, but rather emerge from thoughts, once the perverse effects of mechanical memory free them from reliance on personal meanings. Various elements link together to make coherent wholes. Indeed, Kant's appeal to the principle of sufficient reason suggests how these links work.

We have already discussed the way conditions conspire to generate a sufficient reason. If we transfer this analysis to the way we establish the unity of a complex thought, we may think of the conditions as tendrils of meaning that reach out from the various components. One conditions another; the latter is amenable to being conditioned in some cases, the two mutually condition each other, creating a symbiotic interconnection within the larger thought. Some may specifically orient themselves to each other; others may provide only modifying influences that turn out, on further reflection, to merit revision and correction. In place of a linear, causal sequence, we have a reciprocity of interaction generating complex integrated unities, where the tendrils that bind it together justify each link. In this way, we come to understand the significance of our more intricate thoughts and at times find that they explain why things happen as they do.

Thus we have once again come on the need to consider thoughts not as isolated and independent units, but as notions that, though focused and determinate, none the less contain tendrils reaching out towards other meanings and make possible and exclude one another. The language of conditions provides a way of talking about their influence, since a condition makes other things possible. In the realm of thought, such relations become stronger when conditions reciprocally reinforce one another – when they become, so to speak, a field of mutually interacting forces.

This suggests that there are kinds of tendrils other than those we identified in the previous chapter. Talk of conditions and causes introduces more than simply relations between a genus and its species or the way related contraries exclude each other.

At this point, we do not have much evidence of what these tendrils might be like. For the present, we simply take note of what we have already achieved. We have made some progress towards understanding the way we order our thoughts and look for sufficient conditions to integrate them into larger, more complex unities (as we did with our thought of the exchange rate). This synthetic and integrating activity provides a necessary counterbalance to the analysis of definition. But one feature is missing. In both analysing and unifying, we have been working with pure thoughts on their own as items that we can take apart and combine. But thinking does not happen in isolation. There is a larger context in which it occurs and to which it frequently refers. We need to look at the way reflective thought can do justice to this context and become fully comprehensive.

9

Fourth Rule: Comprehensiveness

IN OUR INVESTIGATION OF THE WAY we clarify thoughts, we have discussed two operations traditionally associated with human reasoning: analysis and synthesis. We take thoughts and break them up into their components; and we combine elements into larger, integrated wholes. In both processes, however, the intellect works with its own products. It views thoughts as functioning in an independent realm, where they develop on their own. But thinking is an activity of beings living in a natural and social world. As such it informs and responds to their interaction with that environment.

To be sure, in our story so far words have their beginnings in ideas; and ideas refer back to immediate impressions and experiences. But mental images and ideas, on their own, cannot escape the spatio-temporal limitations of the particular sensations and experiences where they originated. And the movement to pure thinking involves overcoming that subjectivity and the contingencies of our particular existence. So it is crucial that definition and integration, which render more precise just what our thoughts are, can operate without worrying about what the real world is like.

At this point, however, Descartes's fourth rule becomes significant: "throughout to make enumerations so complete, and reviews so comprehensive, that I could be sure of leaving nothing out." In practice, he seems to have thought that this operation involves nothing more than reflection – an act of pure meditation. But if our review is to be exhaustive and leave nothing out, then we cannot dismiss our interactions with the world around us as irrelevant. A "complete enumeration" would cover how our thoughts fit not just into our limited personal experience, but also into the world as other people experience it and, if possible, into the world as it is in itself.

This task is easier because the development of language has generated an interpersonal realm, where the careful use of definition makes genuine communication possible. We learn from other people who inhabit different spatio-temporal locations about their distinctive experiences, and we share our world of meaning with them. This provides a first step away from the relativity of subjective experience. But it is not enough. Cultures can be as partial as individuals, and civilizations at times come into ideological conflict with each other. While our "enumeration" has reached well beyond the details of our limited past, it does not yet have the capacity to approximate completeness. The world as it is in itself – the world that has an impact on our lives willy-nilly, whether in the past or in the future – has not come into consideration. There needs to be, in principle, some way of reaching beyond the limits of a shared subjectivity.

On first glance, it seems that we humans cannot get outside our own skins. Our only access to the world is through experience – our sensations and intuitions. Even though we share our discoveries with other people, the structure of our species limits all of us – the limited range of sights and sounds, the particular way our nerves process the givens of sense. Even when we use disciplined thought to understand what all this means, the particular beliefs that have emerged in the course of our development restrict us. We interpret the world from our own perspective and fit it into our preconceptions.

In stating this dilemma, however, we have overlooked an important feature of our interaction with the real world. We have talked as if past and present experiences are all that is involved. But we also anticipate the future. Here we do not describe a world already experienced, but predict features that have not yet occurred. Whether they happen as we predict, however, is not within our control. The world as it is in itself impinges on our life; it can confound our most confident expectations. When it confirms our predictions, we may become more confident in our beliefs; but since the enumeration of future events can in principle never be complete, we never achieve absolute certainty.

This interaction with the future can have a significant impact on our thoughts. Success suggests that our beliefs are reliable; failure indicates that something is wrong with them. When the latter happens, we turn our attention back on these thoughts and, with humility, modify our predictions. Over time, we can thus improve their ability to anticipate the way the world functions and free ourselves from the particular prejudices of our human species. By including the future as well as the past in our "enumerations," we can begin to make our thoughts reflect what really is.

C.S. Peirce points out that we do not need to wait until we act on our thoughts to implement this fourth rule. For our reflection is able to work out in advance what kinds of "effects that might conceivably have practical bearings, we conceive the object of our conception to have."[1] The intellect can develop quite detailed predictions of what to expect were we to act on our thoughts. Making our thoughts clear thus involves much more than formulating precise definitions and justifiable interconnections. It includes making predictions about what will happen when we put those thoughts into practice.

The simple act of predicting and putting our expectations into practice may, however, tell us little about the adequacy of our thoughts. We can define the future in so general a way that a wide range of possibilities could satisfy our hopes; and we can always interpret results to fit subjective convictions. The process of prediction can improve the reliability of our thoughts only if we combine it with analysis and integration. When formulating our thought or theory, we need to distinguish it carefully from close competitors and link it up with related operations; then we can focus on experiential tests, where whatever happens will make a significant difference to the success or failure of our expectations. Careful definitions restrict the range of possible effects; justifiable syntheses suggest what correlates we should expect. By articulating our thoughts in this way, we can make our predictions precise enough for future events to make a difference, either establishing their falsity or confirming, for the time being, their reliability. The various operations interact to mutually reinforce each other.

To achieve comprehensiveness, reflection thus turns back to immediate experience. But rather than simply accepting and generalizing from whatever happens, as ideas do, thought structures this encounter. We develop precise expectations, basing them on careful definition and past experience, and then, at an appropriately specified

---

1 C.S. Peirce, "How to Make Our Ideas Clear," in *Collected Papers of Charles Sanders Peirce*, ed. C. Hartshorne and P. Weiss (Cambridge, Mass.: Harvard University Press, 1931–35, 1958), vol. 5, para. 402 (5.402).

time and place, we observe what in fact occurs. By controlling the setting and the specific thoughts we want to explore, we escape many of
the contingencies that bedevil the casual experiences of daily life.
The natural sciences have developed this technique of controlled experimentation in sophisticated ways. But we find it functioning as well
in the practical skills that knowledgeable people develop in many
walks of life – those who work and live with livestock or plant and
maintain gardens, auto mechanics and lumbermen, cooks and weav-
ers, diplomats and social workers. They learn to observe carefully the
results of their actions, and when these are not what they expect,
many reflect humbly on what that tells them about the reliability of
their thoughts. The experience they gain in thus applying their knowledge and skills enables them not only to test out various innovations,
but also to anticipate failures and successes that reach into related
areas they have not yet directly encountered. For all the theoretical
and practical preparation through which these practitioners develop
such expertise, it is through intuitions directly presented to their
senses that they discover the success or failure of their predictions.

A good example of the efficacy of this interaction with the real
world can be found in biology. Since the time of Aristotle, it has
worked with a framework of genus and species that mirrors the components of our definitions. It was based initially on comparative anatomy, and later on whether mating different species could produce
offspring. With the conceptual transformation that emerged with
Darwin's theory of evolution, biologists turned to heredity and common ancestors. Over time, they found that some species are more
closely related than previously thought and that some quite similar
creatures none the less come from quite different ancestors. Comparative anatomy and physiology have led to linking birds and dinosaurs under a single class; yet the eyes of humans and of octopuses,
though remarkably similar, developed long after their lines of heredity had diverged. The discovery and analysis of DNA has refined biological stratification even further. Careful observation and analysis
have made scientists quite uncomfortable with the classifications that
Linnaeus initiated and now form part of the technical names of plants
and animals. Biology is constantly refining the thoughts of genera
and species in the light of prediction and careful observation.

Certain of our thoughts, however, are more independent of the
vagaries of experience, for we use them to organize and structure our
interaction with the world. We distinguish, for example, between an

entity and a process, between a force and a field, between identity and difference, between appearance and reality. Such general conceptions continue to be useful in all our disciplined appeal to experience. Nowhere is this more evident than in mathematics. The fact that we can easily individuate much of what happens into separate things and events enables us to group them into ordered sets that we can enlarge or diminish by adding or removing a member. The sequential links by which we individuate and order numbers quickly prove their value in practice as cultures move from "one, two, and many" to a complete number system. Precision in definition has enabled mathematicians to apply further operations to these thoughts, creating multiples, fractions, square roots, and negative and irrational numbers. A complex system of interconnections has developed, only some of which the world has validated. Surprisingly, physics discovered that the square root of minus one (an irrational number, a seeming contradiction in terms) is an inherent feature of the world in which we live. Careful observation following Einstein's theory of general relativity showed that cosmic space is not Euclidean, as it appears to our everyday experience, but Reimannian.

Other thoughts, however, are not so amenable to experiential checks. The complexity of the world of human affairs, for example, makes it difficult to identify the reason for a failed prediction. We cannot easily set up controlled experiments where only one or two factors fluctuate. And the appeal to statistics in psychology and sociology assumes that we can convert features into countable entities and provides only correlations that admit of exceptions, not exclusive differences. In addition, it can take decades, if not centuries, for all the consequences of putting certain thoughts into practice to take effect. In the interim, many other contingencies and intervening factors come into play, making it difficult to isolate just those benefits and faults that result from implementing the original thought. So it is not easy to ensure that the differentiations and the integrations in our thoughts accurately capture the way things actually work in the world. Historians continue to propose different interpretive explanations for the origins of the world wars, many of which are mutually exclusive.

In the practical realm, we can stipulate how we mean people to understand our thoughts. Governments do this through laws and regulations; but we individuals also do it quite casually in ordinary conversation, or more explicitly in a scholarly treatise. By stipulating the definitions of our terms, we can propose that they retain the same meaning whenever people use them. But this process falls afoul of our human ability to deny and negate. We do not simply adopt, but also react. We call into question the fairness of a law; we challenge the adequacy of a definition by showing exceptions. We proclaim that we should reject and overthrow something that society has unquestioningly accepted.

This results from a peculiar complication in our understanding of human affairs. We are not just applying our thoughts to a reality of a different order – trees and dinosaurs, electrons and microwaves. Our thoughts also shape the reality we are trying to understand. The social world consists of the interaction of many individuals, which relies not only on the use of language, but also on the interpretation of significant behaviour. Human actions are not mere events. They result from intentions – and are full of significance. Meanings and thoughts are thus an intrinsic part of the reality we set out to comprehend. And this makes it difficult to ensure that the terms we are clarifying are not themselves being confounded by the role they play in the social dynamics or even by deliberate attempts by committed individuals and groups to explore excluded contraries. It is thus not as easy to start out with a clear prediction and achieve determinate results in the social sciences of psychology and economics as we do in physics or biology.

None the less we do learn from experience. Wise elders have discovered that certain forms of behaviour are more effective in accomplishing their ends than others; and statesmen who have some sense of the vagaries of history are less confident that their decisions will inevitably move along the path they intend and take more account of the likelihood of contingencies and surprises. The interaction between prediction and result helps define how we use our language in education and politics, and while we may not be as confident in definitions as the natural scientists, we frequently improve our use of language and more carefully consider its practical implications.

While all that we can achieve retains an imprecision that we need to acknowledge – that we work not with certainties but with possibilities and probabilities – it is an achievement nevertheless. We are able to bring to the phenomena of human affairs a way of thinking that sees how actions generate a multitude of tendrils that reach out in all directions and how the links that emerge are products as much of the recipients as of the original intention. At each contact point, a variety of reactions is possible. Understanding this range of possibilities and the likelihood of their coming to fruition is the only way we can hope to be comprehensive, even if we can never fully confirm our predictions. As in the natural sciences, where a failure in prediction suggests the inadequacy of the original thoughts, so in human affairs, such a failure may indicate our blindness to the imprecision and range of possibilities that are part of the complex of thoughts we are investigating.

The close interconnection between thought and action, which complicates our understanding of human affairs, has, however, another implication. It is just our need to act in the world that makes it important to clarify and refine our thoughts. Action requires, first, a clear understanding of our situation. It is not enough to have immediate impressions and images, nor general ideas that can stand for a number of similar instances. We need to understand how the various ingredients of our world in fact connect to each other; we must discover the forces and circumstances that have made the present state of affairs possible. And these conditioning forces resemble the tendrils of significance we discussed in the previous two chapters. To understand the world as it is, we have to ensure that the interconnections among thoughts in our mind match in some appropriate way these conditioning influences in our environment. Even though we can never in human affairs reach the reliability of the natural sciences and mathematics, we should be as realistic and aware of detailed results as a physicist or geologist.

But we also make predictions. We want to introduce changes into the world, whether major or minor, whether we are setting the table for dinner or resolving some conflict among nations. Our action is to have an impact on events. And those events will take place within the world as it is, not as we would like it to be. So, as we deliberate on what action to perform, we should anticipate what would happen were we to do this rather than that. These predictions ought to work out in thought how forces and influences operate in the natural and social world. A proposed action will affect the network of natural and social conditions into which it intrudes. And deliberation needs to think through what to expect and be as comprehensive as possible.

For our thoughts to be fully adequate to our purposes, the network of interconnections that analysis and synthesis reveal cannot be simply the product of pure thought. Thought needs to take account of the way the world is and incorporate into its understanding the tendrils that hold in fact: that maintain things as they are and influence the initiatives we introduce. Only in this way will our thoughts be fully comprehensive.

So, in addition to analysis and synthesis, we have a third step in clarifying our thoughts. We take our thoughts, in all their determinate precision, formulate specific predictions, and use them to inform our actions. Then we see whether the interconnections we have projected actually work out in the way we anticipated. When our predictions are relatively successful, we become more confident about the reliability of our analyses and integrations. If, however, the results surprise us, we must go back to the drawing board and rework the structure of our thoughts.

Hidden in this discussion is an important point. We talked originally about the tendrils that interconnect meanings as if they are a function of pure thought. But we now begin to see interconnections and tendrils that operate among things in the world quite independent of our minds. These are not evident in our immediate experience – neither in the images we retain in our subconscious nor in the imaginative syntheses we may produce as creative poets and in the stream of consciousness. Rather, they emerge as we discover the way our well-thought-out predictions succeed and fail. Successful anticipation reinforces the tendrils connecting various meanings identified by our thoughts; and we come to understand these as links that function within the world. There develops a reciprocal dynamic: the results of our action help to refine the implications of our pure thoughts, even as our thoughts, responding to past experience, enable us to anticipate the interconnections that in fact hold in the world. It is through thoughts trained in this way that we move beyond the booming, buzzing confusion of our immediate sensations and delve ever more deeply below the surface of our experiences into their ultimate significance and nature.

This reciprocal interaction is crucial for our quest to move beyond subjective mental operations and achieve objectivity. Kant claimed that we require a sufficient reason for combining elements into a single, objective concept. Above, I suggested that we work with signs that we draw from the realm of experience and explore the tendrils that connect them to each other. We now find that these tendrils, while functions of our thought, are also functions of the world. It is through the interaction of thought with experience over the long history of human development that humankind has discovered many tendrils that actually function within the world and built them into its thoughts. If we had not moved from ideas to thoughts, we would not realize the significance of what we see and hear; but without the givens of experience, our thoughts would never have emerged from our subjective isolation and verged towards objectivity.

Objectivity in our thinking develops out of our ability to reflect on our thoughts and consider them on their own terms. First, there is a network of conditions that mutually interact to generate sufficient reasons. We can justify why we have developed the particular thoughts we have. Second, this discovery of interconnections is not the function of a single mind. We are able to communicate with each other and, in the resulting discourse, refine our use of terms until we are confident that together we are thinking the same thoughts. Third, we interact with the world in which we live. Our discourse consists not simply of our diverse thoughts, but also of what we have learned from our actions. Through that dynamic interaction, extending over the course of history, we human beings have refined our terms so that they reflect, more or less, the network of interconnections that operate universally.

Where creative imaginations, in a search for novelty, ignore this treasury of accumulated experience and venture out into totally new paths, or where determined agents, anxious to satisfy some pressing desires, impulsively undertake thoughtless initiatives, there is always the danger of failure and disastrous consequences. But where original thought builds on its acquired understanding of how the world operates, and senses where space exists for novel initiatives, humans can move forward, albeit tentatively, into new, as yet unexplored possibilities.

10

Conceiving

WE CAN NOW RETURN TO FREGE'S sharp distinction between ideas and concepts. Concepts, he says, are permanent and independent of the thinking of any one individual. They are objective, and our task is to discover, not generate, them. They thus subsist in some kind of Platonic heaven and are generically different from ideas, which emerge from our experience in response to images and interests that reflect our peculiar circumstances.

To avoid prejudging this claim, I have avoided using the language of concepts in talking about the realm of pure thoughts, for in our story these have emerged out of the realm of ideas. But now, on the basis of our discussion of analysis, synthesis, and comprehensiveness, we can begin to explore how pure thoughts relate to concepts as Frege understands them.

We recall that, for all of Frege's anti-psychologism, he none the less recognizes that grasping a concept involves intellectual activity. Knowledge of other languages can help us; we learn from following false trails; and we benefit from seeing the flaws in the arguments of our predecessors and contemporaries. It can be a matter of great intellectual struggle to come to the point of appropriating subtle and complicated terms. These operations may be functions of our individual minds; none the less, Frege maintains, their purpose is to grasp objective concepts in their eternal purity.

We now have some basis for understanding what grasping concepts involves. We deliberately and self-consciously analyse our thoughts to grasp their precise components and interrelationships. Where we come on inconsistencies, we seek to rectify our mistakes. We take various components and bring them together into integrated unities.

Working with the network of tendrils that extend out from carefully defined thoughts, we construct a pattern in which components mutually condition each other and build up relationships strong enough to justify their union into a single thought. Developing these skills not simply on our own, but in discussion with other people, at times from different languages and cultures, we refine our use of terms so that they begin to escape from the relativism of our personal idiosyncrasies and cultural prejudices. We gradually wean our minds from their personal interests and predilections and become more open to the pure concepts of Frege's ideal. All these operations move us beyond the variability of subjective concerns and enable us to grasp objective thoughts.

But they do more. For we are now left to wonder what remains of Frege's understanding of concepts as subsisting eternally in some sort of Platonic heaven, waiting for disciplined mortal minds to grasp them. Our quest for comprehensiveness has shown that, by using our thinking when we interact with the world, we test out the reliability of the connections our minds construct and revise our understanding in the light of failed expectations. In their interaction over the ages with the natural and social environment, humans have moved beyond the subjectivity of social conventions and shared prejudices. Through this learning process, they have crystallized thoughts that events in the world do not often surprise.

Many of these core thoughts have become permanent fixtures, and our education nurtures us in their reliability. They include the elements of mathematics, as well as many basic principles of agriculture and architecture, fabrics and minerals, trade and commerce. And they include thoughts so fundamental that they permeate virtually all attempts to understand: "quality" and "quantity," "essential" and "accidental," "thing" and "property," "possibility" and "condition." As we have appropriated the learning of the ages, we have moved beyond the contingency of ideas, which we acquired from the immediacy of everyday experience, to understand many basic principles that hold not only for past experience, but also for the future – some indeed as abstract as the square root of minus one. Such thoughts have acquired a permanence that resembles the eternal validity of Frege's concepts.

It seems therefore unnecessary to assume the subsistence of a fixed and permanent realm, lying beyond our minds in a Platonic heaven, waiting for us to fathom. For we have provided a narrative that shows how objective thoughts can gradually escape the contingencies of our "psychological" predilections through operations that are themselves psychological. Our human intellect is able to distance itself from personal interests and meanings and reflect dispassionately on the significance of the terms it uses.

But we have done more. We have established the objectivity of our thoughts not by some intuition into pure concepts, but through our interaction with the world – through carefully delineated predictions, some of which have failed, and others succeeded. Over the centuries, thoughts that had seemed fixed and eternal have turned out to be partial and incomplete. In the social and political realm, unthinkable conceptions have become accepted reality: the participation of all functioning adults, women as well as men, in aspects of government; organizing the infrastructure of our cities to prevent the spread of disease; communicating instantly across vast distances. But similar revolutions have happened in mathematics and science. Until Einstein adopted Reimannian geometry to explain the workings of gravity, scientists assumed that Euclidean geometry presented us with objective concepts that would never come into question. The square root of minus one, which for ages seemed a contradiction in terms, has turned out to be critical in formulating the laws of physics. And Frege's logical attempt to demonstrate conceptually the foundations of arithmetic displayed a fatal flaw. Rather than existing in a realm quite independent of any influence from our human minds, concepts have a history, and that history is a function of careful reflective thought.

Many thoughts have not yet attained the objectivity of concepts. They operate at the frontiers of science, where new discoveries constantly challenge preconceived expectations. And they operate in the field of human affairs, where the contingencies of human passion frustrate the most comprehensive social planning. We find continually the need for new differentiae to discriminate between features that we previously confused. We regularly discover that elements apparently quite unrelated influence the construction of complex unities.

This process of discovery happens at two levels. First, when events surprise us, either in the laboratory or in public life, we reconsider our frames of reference and ask if our thoughts do in fact capture the interconnections in the world. Suddenly aware of new possibilities, our minds begin to suspect distinctions or connections previously missed. But, second, some of the most innovative researchers – those with clear minds and an arsenal of sophisticated thoughts – are able to think back over the material already familiar to their understanding and, simply through reflection, notice links and distinctions they previously overlooked. Exploring these, the likes of Newton and Einstein, Darwin and Adam Smith, have constructed new, complex thoughts that other investigators can then explore through controlled observation in the world. The initiative for modifying pure thoughts comes from both the world of experience and the discipline of trained minds.

To say that earlier thoughts (such as Newton's understanding of a fixed time and space) are not concepts, whereas the most recent ones (such as special relativity) are, simply because eternal concepts cannot be false, begs the question. Frege's claim that concepts are unchanging follows from a too limited focus on the central notions of mathematics and logic – those that have become fixed because they are fundamental to all spheres of human endeavour, the internal functions of the mind as much as the casual encounters with an external world. It allows no place for the rich range of significant thoughts that the natural and social sciences advance in explanatory hypotheses and gradually modify in the light of practical experience of the world. None of these can claim infallibility; they are always open to revision and reconsideration. To claim that such precise thoughts, because they are subject to modification and change, are not concepts seems perverse. They frequently play the same role in our ongoing investigations as those that are more permanent. And some of them gradually move from being somewhat hypothetical to unquestioned acceptance. There seems no reason to hold that, at such moments, they are changing their ontological status. Even as reflection refines their precision, they are none the less sufficiently determinate to allow a conceptual exploration of their objective implications.

In other words, we have come to the point where we can say to Frege: we have no need of your hypothesis. We can do justice to the explanatory power of concepts and their relative independence of individual mental histories without abandoning their foundation within the natural world in which we live – the world in which we perceive and think, where we succeed and fail, and where mountains tremble and political revolutions erupt. Concepts are those thoughts that people have refined by careful analysis, deliberate and controlled use of sufficient reason, careful observation of the ways their thoughts play out in the world, sensitive awareness of those forces that frustrate their expectations, and constructive dialogue among reflective thinkers across many cultures and generations. As these operations have modified and reinforced each other over the course of human history, their thoughts have acquired an objectivity that satisfies all the features of Frege's concepts. There is no need to leap into another genus.

Frege's use of the term "psychologism" led him astray. In thrall to the obvious variability that we find in our ideas and the images that accompany them, he decided that all mental activity must be unreliable. But, in our analysis, we have suggested that human psyches have a significant self-reflexive capacity he overlooks: we can become aware of limitations in our thoughts, take account of them, and deliberately adjust our operations and functions to overcome them.

Through mechanical memory, we free ourselves from reliance not only on retained images, but also on the personal meanings we associate with words. Through disciplined reflection, we analyse and construct concepts, discount contingencies, and develop strong unities. Through public discourse, we test out our thoughts within the larger arena of human society, which stretches back through the ages of human history and moves forward into an immediate future. And through initiatives and observations in the world of anticipated experience, we learn which of our thoughts fit with the ongoing dynamic of our world. All these operations happen within the psyches of individual persons – what we have called their "minds."

The discipline of psychology may well investigate the role they play in the construction of concepts. But that does not mean that particular experiences and subjective interests unavoidably affect all the resulting thoughts – that grasping the concepts that logic uses is a process that we should cast out into the waste bin of subjective relativism. Deliberate reflection uses tools by which it transcends partiality and overcomes the limitations that restrict our understanding. In other words, concepts as well as ideas are the result of psychological processes. We can draw a significant distinction between them: ideas happen and respond to unnoticed influences; concepts are the product of careful reflection and disciplined observation. None the less both function within our minds.

As we saw above, concepts are not atomic units. Each one contains tendrils that open up connections to other thoughts. We become aware of them through movements that happen in the mind. These moves are not conditioned by the contingencies of past experience – the laws of association – but are the result of careful reflection. They stem from the way we define our terms; they justify the integration of various thoughts into more complex unities; and they have been modified through our disciplined interaction with the world.

The tendrils of thought are as independent of our personal histories as the concepts in which they inhere. Following through an implication is not a chance subjective sequence, but emerges through careful reflection and disciplined observation. So when, in thinking a thought, our minds move to a related term – its contrary, its genus, or its constituent species; its condition, its complement, or its predictable consequences – we are not tracing a subjective and arbitrary path. For all that it happens within our psyches, this move is not "psychological" in Frege's sense. Deliberate reflection forms it; it is verging towards objectivity.

We introduce caution into that last statement because of the inherent fallibility of our beliefs. We may have achieved much in comprehending the world, but events continue to surprise us, not only in human affairs, but also in science. Objectivity, it turns out, is not an all-or-nothing state of affairs; it is open to gradations of comprehensiveness. For all that concepts and their tendrils are objective, they cannot guarantee absolute truth.

Mediating between ideas and concepts lies the realm of pure thoughts. In the story I have been developing, these are distinct from concepts. Pure thoughts are those words and senses that are separated both from the images of our normal ideas and from personal meanings. As such, they can be imprecise and vague – raw material for investigation and experiential application, but as yet too inchoate to be objective; they are amenable to refinement. Concepts, in contrast, are determinate enough that we can draw precise implications from their meanings. Because they have emerged from disciplined reflection, public discourse can identify and justify their components and internal relations.

Indeed, we should probably distinguish between "reflection," where thought refines its terms on the way to fully developed concepts, and "conceiving," or the activity of disciplined thinking that works simply with the tendrils and implications of meaning. Both are operations of the mind, and thus psychological; both involve freeing the mind from subjective and relative perspectives; but only the latter can claim some measure of objectivity The first thinks back over the way thoughts function to free the mind from partiality. The second takes seriously the inherent meaning of a term and explores the tendrils that flow out from it. Within the interpretive structure I have adopted, concepts become just one delimited species within the larger genus of pure thoughts, just as all such thoughts, as well as the intuitions, images, and ideas we discussed above, are distinct species within a larger genus that we might call "intellectual representations."

With this conclusion, I have come to the end of my initial puzzle. I have responded to Frege's dualism of ideas and concepts by showing how we can understand them as stages on a continuum of intellectual operations that extends from immediate sensation to rigorous logical investigation. And I have suggested that, when our minds move from one notion to another, they need not be simply drawing on past experiences, which our subjectivity conditions, but responding to tendrils that are inherent in the terms themselves.

PART TWO

Tendrils of Thought

IN PART II, I EXPAND ON SOME THEMES that I have adumbrated in part I of this book. Of critical importance is the role of what I have called 'tendrils.' That metaphor suggests, but does not explain and clarify, what is involved: it remains in the realm of ideas. To explore their role in a fully satisfactory way is, at the present time, beyond my capacities. But I can develop some themes that may give it more plausibility and provide the basis for further investigation.

One particular path I shall not follow. In our discussion of comprehensiveness, I talked about the way both disciplined science and informed experience make us aware of new kinds of tendrils in the world and build them into the concepts we use to explain and advise. Philosophers and historians of science have explored many of the advances that have shattered explanatory models and replaced them with more comprehensive theories. It would need extensive knowledge of this history, and a detailed understanding of the significance of 'paradigm shifts,' to trace the way the discoveries of both thought and experiment have incorporated new tendrils of meaning into conceptual thought. While I have provided some examples of how this has happened, I do not have the competence to do this with a thorough and satisfactory narrative. So, with regret, I must leave that task to others.

I turn instead to the question of how conceptual thought on its own can ascertain and investigate the way thoughts reach out to establish connections with each other. Four approaches to this topic suffice. First, I start by returning, in chapter 11, to Hegel. He did, after all, serve as the occasion for my initial interest in psychologism. I questioned Frege's dualism because of my conviction that,

in the *Science of Logic,* Hegel is examining what happens when we
conceive. On my reading of this difficult and dense text, one starts
from relatively inchoate and imprecise terms (Hegel would call
them 'indeterminate') and gradually explores the implicit meanings
– the tendrils – that lead not only to other terms, but eventually to
more fully refined concepts. By looking at one example of how he
does this, we can obtain some sense of the role tendrils play when
we conceive.

Second, I consider what the traditional forms of inference can
tell us about the way tendrils connect one concept to another.
Arguments are designed to draw out implications, making what is
implicit explicit. In other words, there are tendrils in the premises
that justify the move to the conclusion. Even though formal logic
removes all conceptual content to focus simply on argument forms,
these forms themselves retain implicit links that ground their legitimacy. Why did the Aristotelian syllogism become the standard of all
reasoning for centuries (see chapter 12)? What makes *modus ponens*
such a powerful device in modern symbolic logic (chapter 13)?
I attempt to answer these questions by exploring the tendrils
implicit in these two logical forms.

Third, when looking for creative solutions of conceptual puzzles,
we frequently fall back on the much-less-rigorous form of argument
from analogy. Because it compares the way different sets of things
relate to each other, it presupposes the significance of networks of
linkages. Although the inferences are not as objective as the previous two forms, they are none the less productive. In chapter 14, we
explore some of the reasons for their usefulness.

Fourth, in chapter 15, I examine the way the syntax of a language
provides a distinctive framework for tendrils that can be exploited
when developing explanatory hypotheses.

I conclude with two general observations. In the first (chapter 16),
I consider the way ideas and concepts interact in our daily lives;
in the second (Epilogue), I suggest, rather tentatively, some metaphysical implications that follow from the story I have advanced.

11

Hegel's Logic

AS FAR AS I KNOW, Hegel is the only philosopher who has system-atically examined what happens when we conceive in a disciplined way. In his *Science of Logic*, he traces a series of successive intellectual operations that lead on from one to another. That narrative does not follow a phenomenal history, describing events in some stream of consciousness, but rather lays out the sequence of concepts that emerge as we thinking beings, nurtured by the wisdom of the ages and our experience of the world, follow tendrils of thought. It re-counts what happens within the objective realm of concepts, yet finds expression in disciplined thinking.

Immanuel Kant was the first to claim that there are fundamental categories of all thought that determine how we understand the world. When he wanted to justify his choice of twelve basic functions, he appealed to the traditional forms of logical propositions. Hegel, unhappy with this approach, believed that we could derive categories of thought only from thought itself. And so he initiated a new under-taking: "to set out the realm of thoughts philosophically." By "philo-sophically," he meant showing the realm "in its proper, immanent activity, or (which is the same thing) in its necessary development."[1] When we think each category on its own, we will be led on to others that follow from it.

Hegel could assume that the categories of his *Logic* are central to all human discourse because he had already tackled the demand of

---

1 Preface to 2nd ed., my translation. See *Hegel's Science of Logic*, trans. A.V. Miller (London: Allen & Unwin, 1969), 31; G.W.F. Hegel, *The Science of Logic*, trans. G. di Giovanni (Cambridge: Cambridge University Press, 2010), 11–12.

comprehensiveness in an earlier work, the *Phenomenology of Spirit*. In that volume, he traces a sequence of experiences where confident claims to knowledge are put forward only to be proved inadequate and contradictory in practice, forcing revision. As the knowledge claims become more sophisticated, they not only range more widely but also become more self-reflective. Hegel's conclusion is that all knowledge whatever involves a process of claim, failure, and reworking – the dynamic I described in chapter 9 above on comprehensiveness.[2] When he turns to the *Logic*, his focus on thought assumes that the concepts and categories he explores have emerged from the accumulated experience of individuals and of our species generally. So he can limit himself to the 'immanent activities' proper to thought itself: analysis and synthesis, or (in our terms) definition and integration.

An example from the *Logic* provides a good illustration of the way tendrils of thought lead from concept to concept. I focus on a single text: his discussion of the concepts 'finite' and 'infinite.'[3] And I use the language of tendrils to throw light on its development. However, Hegel follows no single path. For he revised the passage extensively just before he died; and the summary *Encyclopaedia Logic*, written as a textbook for his lectures, adopts a different itinerary, which is quite a bit shorter. It would seem that, while he does hold that tendrils lead us from thought to thought, he is not saying that there is only one route to follow. Conceptual thought may move in different ways, depending on the detail or particular focus of the thinker, without thereby compromising its objectivity.

I start with the term 'finite.' Something finite has been defined as a qualified and determinate being. Were any of its determinations to disappear and give way to others, that finite something becomes something else. Thus there are limits to what it can be. Something is finite because it has a limit beyond which it cannot go without ceasing to be itself.

---

2 I argue for this understanding of absolute knowledge in chapter 5 of my *Hegel's Systematic Contingency* (Basingstoke: Palgrave Macmillan, 2007). On the general thesis of this paragraph, see chapter 4 of my *The Logic of Hegel's Logic* (Peterborough: Broadview, 2006).

3 In *On Hegel's Logic* (Atlantic Highlands, NJ: Humanities, 1981), I develop this kind of analysis for eight chapters of the *Science of Logic*. Other chapters I consider in detail in *Real Process* (Toronto: University of Toronto Press, 1996) and *Hegel's Systematic Contingency*. Throughout this discussion, I use single quotes to indicate the conceptual meanings that are in question.

This definition is the result of drawing together a number of tendrils of thought. It distinguishes 'a being' from 'being in general' by some indeterminate qualification.[4] That differentia introduces the thought of 'quality'; and when we link 'quality' with the original 'being,' we have the thought of 'a qualified being.' This synthetic move is justifiable because a 'quality' is not an independent monad of thought but incorporates the tendril of 'inhering in something else'; so not only does 'a being' imply a 'quality,' but any 'quality' entails some 'being' in which it inheres. Were we then, using what Kant has called our "understanding," to collapse the complex sense, 'a qualified being,' with its pair of reciprocal tendrils, into a single, unified concept, the name we would normally choose for the result is 'something.'

The concept 'something' has its own tendrils. As soon as we say, for example, that 'some' leaves are green, we directly move on to thinking of the 'other' leaves that were ignored. Just as 'some' in this concrete example leads over to the thought of 'others,' so the abstract thought of 'something' follows implicit tendrils that lead to the thought of 'other.' Such a transition, from 'something' to 'something else,' involves a process that we can conceive as an 'alteration' or 'becoming other' – a term that applies as well to the movement that has taken place in our thinking. We have thus generated a new thought that we need to explore.

For 'alteration' to take place, that which determines something as distinctive must disappear and some other determination emerge. In our example, the green changes to some alternative colour such as red, brown, or yellow. In the abstract terms of pure thought, this means that any 'something' has a specific 'determination' that both identifies its particular being and differentiates it from any other into which it might change. When we want to define a particular determination of something, however, we consider not only its specific inherent quality, but also how that character is determined or 'constituted' – including that out of which it comes and into which it goes. In other words, a 'determination' sets a 'limit' beyond which 'something' ceases to be. And by putting the result of this thinking together with the term from which we started, we arrive at 'a limited something,' our original definition for 'finite.'

---

4 To maintain some sense of colloquial English, I am using 'a being' for Hegel's *Dasein*.

In the argument so far, we have found that tendrils play a crucial role. The difference between 'a being' and 'pure being' leads over to 'quality' and 'qualification.' This last term cannot function entirely on its own but requires a reciprocal relationship with 'a being.' 'Something' leads to 'other,' a transition that we call 'alteration'; and any 'alteration' contains within it tendrils that require the thoughts of an 'inherent determination,' the 'constituting' influence of the related others, and 'limit.' But these three terms function only because of their links with the original 'something.' Integrating that reciprocal relationship leads us to 'finite.'

The tendrils have become evident as our thoughts move from a term to its opposite or correlate. Though taking place in our minds, these transitions none the less respond not to idiosyncratic experiences and associations, but to aspects inherent in the meanings we are thinking. They have been built into the way those concepts are defined relative to other thoughts and terms.

Hegel's discussion does not stop there. Thought then explores the tendrils implicit in the concept 'finite.' Its specific determination as 'something' positively defines what it 'is to be.' But this means that its negative 'limit' becomes a 'barrier' beyond which this 'being' cannot go if it is to fulfil this destiny. In return, the positive sense also becomes stronger as what that thing 'ought to be.' It is understood as some kind of impulsion that pushes up against the barrier and tries to get beyond it. When we refine the elements of the definition of 'finite,' we expose a radical tension between 'barrier' and 'ought' – one that generates new kinds of tendrils that reach out towards other meanings.

The 'ought' strives to go beyond the 'limit'; but the latter, as 'barrier,' entails that whatever is beyond is other than the 'finite'; but the contrary of 'finite' is 'infinite.' So we have arrived at the thought of 'infinity' in the elementary sense of something indefinite that lies 'beyond' finitude.

When our thinking actually goes beyond any definite limit, however, it arrives not at something totally indeterminate, but at a thought itself defined by its contrast with the original finite – its opposite. So this infinite 'beyond' turns out to be limited by its contrary and so paradoxically satisfies our original definition of 'finite' as a limited something. This new 'finite' in its turn undergoes the same process, pushing 'beyond' its limit to a new 'infinite,' which then turns out to be determinate and 'finite,' and so on, *ad infinitum*.[5] When we reflect back on this whole repetitive dynamic, we notice that we have come up with a second sense of the thought 'infinite.' In addition to the sense of a 'beyond,' we now have the thought of an 'infinite process' (or regress), in which each newly emerging finite thing moves beyond its limit to become something else.[6]

An infinite regress of this sort has its own peculiar characteristics. Each 'beyond' that we supposed to be the opposite of the finite, and so infinite, turns out to be itself finite. Yet the finite does not disappear but continues to emerge, 'persisting' as a permanent feature of the dynamic, and to that extent is unlimited or infinite. Thus a third sense emerges: the 'infinite' can now mean what continues to 'persist' for all its limitations. In the infinite regress, then, we have a network of thoughts, in which the thought of 'finite' leads over to the thought of 'infinite' both in the sense of a 'beyond' and in that of its own persistence; while the thought of 'infinite' leads over to the thought of 'finite' both because it is 'limited' by its opposite and because it is continually striving to become what it 'ought to be.'

At this point, suggests Hegel, we can call on conceptual thought to reflect on the pattern as a whole. What we have is a double process in which the thought of 'finite' and the thought of 'infinite' reciprocally lead over to each other. In the one, we have an indefinite, but repetitive progress moving from 'limited' to 'beyond' and back to 'limited.' In the other, we find that both terms, on their own, transmute into their opposites: the 'infinite beyond' is in fact 'finite,' and the 'limited finite' never in fact disappears and is thus 'infinite.' We have a complex thought in which defining what makes 'finite' and 'infinite' distinct from each other turns out to require a network of mutual implications in which each one has tendrils that embrace and entangle the other. They are bound together in a synthesis – a comprehensive dynamic that moves back and forth: at once establishing the necessity of each term and then immediately recognizing that it

5 In one of his shorter scenarios, Hegel says that, since the 'beyond' of the 'infinite' is the 'finite,' we have generated a reciprocal interaction that can be called the 'valid infinite.' In the larger *Logic*, he takes a much longer route to the same end.

6 This is not the infinite regress of the number system (which Hegel discusses in a later section of his work), but an unlimited qualitative series in which any finite or limited entity inevitably passes away to become something else.

entails its opposite. By reflecting on that network of meanings, we soon recognize that we can call the whole process 'infinite' in yet another sense, since this complex process is fully self-determining and involves nothing outside it that would influence or limit it. We have come on a fourth sense of the term.

Hegel's full analysis of the concept 'infinite' is more complex than I suggest here. But even in this abbreviated version, we can see that he has come up with at least four quite different senses of the term 'infinite': 'beyond,' 'regress,' 'persistence,' and 'self-perpetuating reciprocity.' The four senses emerge progressively from our definition of the 'finite' as we exploit the tendrils within it: both the 'ought to be' and the 'barrier.' The first sense is what is on the other side of the barrier; the second emerges from the dynamic as we find ourselves moving back and forth from one sense to the other; the third recognizes the way finitude continues to reappear even as it is supposed to be transcended and the fourth considers the pattern of reciprocal implication as a whole.

Which one of these four senses would satisfy Frege's requirement of a thoroughly objective thought that remains eternal and unmoved, independent of our thinking as "psychological"? Our analysis suggests that such a question is misplaced. Each one of these senses is not some retained image, with its experiential associations, but the result of a process of thinking about pure meanings and their implications. And we may use each one of them when describing a particular state of affairs. The initial 'beyond' results from working out in detail what is meant by 'finite' and matches our sense of transcendence. The second sense, of 'infinite progress or regress,' is nothing but the recognition that the transition from one to another is in principle repeatable for ever and captures the dynamic of transient events in the world of nature and human affairs. The third sense – of persistence – comes from considering how the 'finite' continues to re-emerge even when it is transcended and matches our sense of the eternal that is somehow independent of transient changes. And the fourth simply steps back and considers how the two terms 'infinite' and 'finite' mutually define each other in a single, reciprocal dynamic and could identify the richness of the universe or indeed of any self-perpetuating and self-contained dynamic.

It may be tempting to take this final, reciprocal interaction of 'infinite' (sense 1) and 'finite' as the pure and proper sense of 'infinite.' Hegel indeed calls it the 'valid' or 'genuine infinite,' in contrast to the 'bad infinites' of the beyond, the regress, and the persistence. But its sense is not independent of those earlier definitions. It presup-. poses and incorporates them into its own complex unity. Each of these four concepts is the result of rigorous investigation of thoughts and of their tendrils and interconnections. They do not exist in a realm of eternity apart from the dynamic of pure thinking. But they are also not prey to the particular associations and past experiences of the thinker. They have resulted from what has happened over time as humans have refined thoughts and explored tendrils with disciplined and perceptive minds.

Hegel makes a final move, which introduces a peculiar way that tendrils can function. At the end of his chapter, thought reflects on the final, complex sense of 'infinite.' As we saw above, it involves the reciprocal relationship by which the thought of 'finite' has tendrils leading over to and engulfing the thought of 'infinite,' and vice versa. The whole conceptual pattern is a self-contained and reciprocal interaction. At the same time, it remains only a synthesis of a number of interacting parts, each of which is defined as both limited and enduring. By adopting Kant's suggestion that conceiving, in its proper sense, transforms syntheses into unities, Hegel takes this complex thought and collapses it into a single, simple concept. This is the thought of something self-contained, or fully determinate on its own account. To provide this new thought with a name, Hegel calls on the German expression "being for itself," which, unfortunately, does not have a natural equivalent in English.[7] By so doing, Hegel moves beyond the dialectic that led us from a simple 'qualified being' to the 'infinite' and introduces a new conceptual term with its own tendrils and implications.

This final move, which unites reciprocal transitions into a new, integrated concept, is peculiar to Hegel. It does not surface easily whenever we reflect on the way our mind thinks through a problem. Yet we should not dismiss it too quickly. It captures in thought a

---

7 Although in some circumstances we might talk of something being "of itself."

dynamic relationship we have already come across in our discussion of language. We appropriate a common language, we agreed, through reciprocal interactions with people around us. Indeed, we went further: "This mutual give-and-take can, in due course, settle into a pattern that develops a character of its own. The unity that emerges is then free to interact with its environment, not merely as a collection of independent units, but as an integrated agent." Reciprocal interaction that collapses into a simple unity can be found, I suggested, not only in our conceptual reasoning but also in our social lives and even in biology. Hegel's intellectual move from reciprocity to integration may in fact capture a central feature of much causal interaction in our world.

But enough of this example from his *Logic*. It has suggested how thought explores tendrils implicit in definitions and how it moves from concept to concept without recourse to subjective images or idiosyncratic ideas. Hegel, however, is not everyone's cup of tea. Even though the language of tendrils can make sense of his logical argument, it would not impress many readers. Yet they also appeal to implications in their own reasoning. This is why I now turn to considering some standard forms of argument.

12

Syllogisms

ARISTOTLE WAS THE FIRST PHILOSOPHER to examine how we move from one thought to another. Reasoning, he said, involves a pattern through which two sentences lead on to a third. By classifying sentences into four types, he identified a number of possible structures, of which, it turns out, only a handful involve a legitimate inference. By identifying the constraints that limit the number of possible transitions within his logical schema, we may throw more light on the tendrils that connect concept to concept.

Aristotle starts by linking concepts together into judgments; and he reduces all judgments to one basic form "S is P," coupling a subject term with a predicate. Sometimes, there is a connecting word, or copula: "Mary is clever"; or "Roses are flowers"; or "Ulan Bator is the capital of Mongolia." But the verb is not strictly necessary; some languages indicate the relation simply by having the qualifier follow the subject (predicative, as in "Mary clever") rather than precede it (attributive, as in "clever Mary").

Aristotle then divides judgments into affirmative or negative, depending on the copula – whether they assert or deny the link; and into particular or universal, depending on whether they include all, or only some, instances of the subject term. So he is able to reduce the number of predicative forms to four: All S are P (universal affirmative); Some S are P (particular affirmative); No S is P (universal negative); and Some S are not P (particular negative). Since terms can serve as either subject or predicate in a judgment, and all inferences involve two premises that share a common term and a conclusion that couples the remaining two terms, there are 256 possible syllogisms. Only a few of these, however, justify an inference.

The predicate can take a number of forms. Aristotle himself real-
ized that it could indicate a quality, a state, or the quantity of the
subject, its location in space or time, or indeed a relation. (Being a
capital, for example, relates Ulan Bator to Mongolia.) Many cou-
plings provide a means for telling others what has gone on within the
subjective stream of our consciousness: the way several distinctive
qualities have come together in our experience, similarities that we
have noticed, the number of times an event has been repeated,
names that signify things, and creative metaphors. But none of these
carries the objectivity that we expect (and Frege demands) of concepts. Inference needs to move from concept to concept with some
reliability. Since it cannot rely on subjective associations, it must draw
on some tendrils of conceptual meaning that legitimately connect
one thought to another. In discriminating between justifiable and
unjustifiable inferences, Aristotle has to separate predications that
articulate conceptual necessity from descriptions of happenstance.

It turns out that, in all successful arguments, at least one premise
has to be a universal: either All S is P or No S is P. The most useful
among this select company are the "Barbara" syllogism: "All humans
are mortal; dictators are human; so dictators are mortal"; and
"Celarent": "No squirrels are carnivores; all the creatures in our back-
yard are squirrels; so no creature in our back yard could have eaten
the pigeon."

There is, however, a problem with universal predications. It is difficult to generate them from the realm of ideas deriving from personal experience; since these are always conditioned by the time and
place in which they occur, they can never ensure that all instances of
a thing will be the same. Only if we delimit a set in some way and then
count every single member of that set, can we hope to claim that *all*
instances of the subject term have (or do not have) the same predicate. But because the arbitrary way we delimit our set has reintro-
duced subjectivity, there can be no guarantee, even then, that we
have created an objective universal. It would be idiosyncratic to restrict our options in this way.

Universals, however, do emerge from the way we define our concepts. As we saw in chapter 7 above, we first identify a more general
context and then differentiate a particular meaning from others that
it might cover. This means that every instance where the particular
concept applies is included within the more general context. A

universal affirmative judgment is appropriate: "All dogs are animals." At the same time, definition differentiates a concept by excluding other possible alternatives. This provides a basis for universal negative judgments: "No maples are oaks."

So it is not surprising that Aristotelian science works with the vocabulary of genus and species. It identifies individuals in terms of their species and organizes species by their relationships with each other within more general types, or genera. Since the world of nature appears to have a hierarchy similar to the one we find within our concepts, the Aristotelian syllogism provides a structure within which we can objectively identify the way things are and how they relate to one another.

As long as the concepts we use have precise definitions, as in mathematics or law, and as long as these definitions specify what features of individual things identify actual instances, we can employ concepts to develop a strict and logical interrelationship. But when we move beyond this to the world of experience, problems arise. How do we identify the species of a particular thing? What is the genus within which it sits? And what other excluded species occur within this genus? Aristotle believed that there was a "look," or (in Latin) *species*, which identifies the species (or conceptual description) of the things we encounter. But once science has shown that the look of things often deceives us, this assumption ceases to be plausible.

In response, logicians then appealed to induction – the reasoning that goes from a number of particular examples to a universal – from "some" to "all." This kind of inference, however, confronts a fundamental problem. We may be able to exhaustively list all the cases that have occurred in the past, but that can provide no certainty about the future. It is always possible that we may encounter a situation where the supposed universal does not apply. The standard illustration is the surprise of Europeans when, believing that all swans were white, they encountered the black swans of Australia.

Scientists have refined their analysis of existing cases to reduce some of the problems with induction and make their concepts more comprehensive. John Stuart Mill sketched out the basic principles of their approach. This method adapts the two contrary moments of identity and difference that are central to the process of definition, formulates them as agreement and disagreement, and uses them in the analysis of situations and events that occur in our experience. Every experience consists of a number of factors. If, on looking at a specific number of cases, we find that one feature, B, is always present when A is present, even though other aspects vary considerably; and if, whenever B is absent, A also is absent, even though other aspects are similar, we have reason to believe that, in general, whenever A is present B will be present; or All As are Bs. To establish a universal negative ("No As are Bs"), one needs to vary the circumstances in the set of cases as much as possible and find that A's presence always co-incides with B's absence and A never appears when B is around. Using this kind of careful observation of past events, one has a rea-sonable conviction that the universal judgments are justifiable.[1]

Thus, over time, we learn from our successes or failures how to refine our concepts until they comprehensively capture relationships within the world. The general term "animal" includes as its particular subcomponents birds, fish, insects, mammals, marsupials, and rep-tiles, even though none of these subgroups overlap; "mammals" in-cludes dogs and humans and mice, for all that they are mutually exclusive; and "dogs" includes great Danes and retrievers and spaniels, although in this case hybrids show that we cannot easily in-troduce universal negative judgments. By carefully observing how characteristics are present or absent in a wide variety of cases, we make our universal judgments comprehensive, ensuring that they capture the relationships that are inherent in the world. We can con-fidently make universal affirmations: Fido is a spaniel; all spaniels are dogs; all dogs are mammals; and all mammals are animals; and uni-versal negations: no dogs are mice; no mammals are insects; no flow-ers are animals. We discover relationships that can be built into conceptual definitions.

As we apply Mill's methods more comprehensively, looking for wider and wider ranges of diversity when seeking agreement, or more extensive ranges of comparability while searching for disagreement, we can ensure the objectivity of our definitions – that they fit the world in which we live. Once we have transformed them into con-cepts by careful observation and disciplined reflection, we can begin

---

1 Mill, *A System of Logic, Ratiocinative and Inductive* (London: Longmans, 1961), Book III, Chapter viii. Mill lists four "methods," but they are basically variations of the themes I mention here.

to adopt and apply Aristotle's forms of valid argument. The syllogisms presuppose tendrils implicit in the process of definition.

This means, however, that the Aristotelian syllogism has a very limited conceptual use. Unfortunately, its logical strength has made it an attractive rhetorical tool for use in public discourse, where the terms "all" and "none" receive a much less precise sense: "All Canadians pay taxes; no one wants to pay more taxes; so everyone wants taxes to be reduced." Such statements draw on the universal sense of the logical terms to make their case plausible. However, when challenged, the speaker will probably admit that a new-born infant or someone with a serious handicap pays no tax and that there are many citizens willing to pay higher taxes if that will ensure reliable bridges, efficient health care, effective law enforcement, and competent educational institutions. In such situations, the speaker is not using the critical words in their strict, definitional sense, but more vaguely and impressionistically. And that can lead to unwise and inappropriate initiatives. Syllogisms can use hasty generalizations to justify any number of contrary proposals. The rhetorical use of "all" and "none" is designed to veil critical reflection that would expose the imprecision of the concepts used.

It is extremely difficult to establish a reliable and objective universal. When rendering our concepts fully comprehensive, we can seldom fit them into definitional hierarchies; we invoke instead statistical probabilities and supposed likelihoods. By that time, however, the tendrils of strict implication have become much more tenuous.

So the Aristotelian syllogism, applying forms of predication, leads us back to our earlier discussion of how we define concepts – through analysis into genus and species – and to our concern for comprehensiveness. Where we use Aristotle's judgment forms for contingent relationships that reflect particular occasions or places, inferences are unreliable. Only when we test our experiences with Mill's methods of agreement and disagreement can we hope for some kind of objective reliability; then our thoughts begin to approximate the hierarchical structures of concepts that range from the most general to the most specific in an ordered sequence of genus and species. All members of a species can fit into a genus. No member of a species is included in any of the alternative species that complete that level of analysis.

Unfortunately, Aristotle's whole system of syllogistic inference cannot easily tell us anything that we did not already know, at least in principle. To establish the reliability of the universal premises as exhaustive, either including or excluding all the representatives of the subject term, we have to show it to be a concept that includes as part of its inherent meaning the tendrils that bond it to its genus and differentiate it from other species. But that renders the question of its particular application in the syllogism virtually redundant.

13

Modus ponens et al.

THE ONLY MAJOR CHANGE IN THE logic of inference after Aristotle came from the Stoics. They took conditionals, such as "If it is raining, then the streets are wet," or disjunctions, such as "Either she stayed home, or she went to the store," and used them as the first premises of inference. In a second premise, one could affirm the antecedent of the conditional ("It is raining") and conclude, "The streets are wet." Or one could deny the consequent ("The streets are not wet"), leading to "It is not raining." Starting from a disjunction, the strongest inference was from the denial of one of the disjuncts ("She did not go to the store") to the affirmation of the other ("She stayed home"), although in certain cases affirmation of one might imply denial of the other.

In these arguments, the units are not concepts or terms, but complete judgments, which could be the predications that Aristotle favoured ("Streets are wet"), or sentences built around active verbs ("She went to the store"). What generates the move from premise to conclusion is not the content of those judgments but the complex structures *if-then* and *either-or*, both of which conjoin two or more propositions. One can exploit these in a variety of ways, starting with those we saw above: *modus ponens*, or affirming the antecedent; *modus tollens*, or denying the consequent; and the disjunctive syllogism. One can also connect two conditionals to produce a hypothetical syllogism ("If it is raining, then the streets are wet"; "If the streets are wet, then they will be slippery"; "So if it is raining, then the streets are slippery"). Or one can combine a disjunction with two conditionals to create what is called a dilemma ("Either she already had some bread or she went to the store"; "If she already had some bread, it is likely stale"; "If she went to the store, she is tired"; or "So either she probably has stale bread or she is tired").

Since it is the conceptual content of *if-then* and *either-or* that generates all these inferences, it is worth focusing on what they imply. A conditional says that, whenever a certain situation occurs, another distinct event will take place. There is a necessary and inevitable connection that leads from one to the other; although the antecedent need not actually happen, the two states of affairs take place in an inevitable sequence. A disjunction says that there are two or more alternatives and that they exhaust all possibilities. Those alternatives may exclude each other, or they may all be possible together.

What are the tendrils, implicit in conditionals and disjunctions, that link antecedent to consequent, or disjunct to disjunct? What justifies the objective necessity of the logic that uses them to move from premises to conclusion? The demand that our concepts be comprehensive makes it imperative that we look not simply at an analysis of the definitions of the terms, but also at the way successful predictions in the world have justified them. To tackle such questions, it is helpful to go back into the past and see how people originally used conditionals and disjunctions and how these types of sentences entered the structure of formal logic.

An early use of these forms in argument appears in dilemmas. A couple of examples may be useful:

Jesus once asked his interlocutors: "Was the baptism of John from heaven or from men?" And they discussed it with one another, saying, "If we say, 'From heaven,' he will say, 'Why did you not believe him?' But if we say, 'From men,' all the people will stone us; for they are convinced that John was a prophet." So they answered that they did not know whence it was. (Luke 20: 4–7)

Diodorus Cronus (d. 284 BCE) receives credit for the following argument for fatalism: "If it is true that there will be a sea battle tomorrow, then nothing can prevent it; and if it is false that there will be a sea battle tomorrow, then nothing can cause it. It is either true that there will be a sea battle tomorrow or false that there will be a sea battle tomorrow. Therefore nothing can prevent the sea battle or nothing can cause the sea battle."

Both cases present an exclusive alternative. Jesus' question poses one; the other assumes that truth and falsity are contradictory. Each one of the alternatives carries with it a specific implication – a tendril that works out from the original thought. This builds either on the basic sense of what the antecedent says or on consequences that experience suggests likely. These conditionals then license the conclusion, which is a new, disjunctive alternative.

There were two standard ways of challenging a dilemma. One proves that the alternatives – the "horns" of the dilemma – are not exhaustive and that there are other options. Aristotle, for example, replied to Diodorus by saying that statements about future events are neither true nor false. This approach – "escaping through the horns" – challenges the truth of the disjunction. Or one could show that the implications are not strictly necessary – that the antecedents need not lead on to the consequent. This approach – "grasping the horns" – denies the truth of the conditionals. These standard rebuttals isolate the sense that is critical to each form of judgment. A disjunction has to be exhaustive; and the sequence in the conditional must always happen whenever the antecedent occurs. These conditions are the tendrils that make *modus ponens* and its fellows work.

Because it is so difficult to establish either a necessary sequence or an exhaustive listing, early logicians paid little attention to arguments using these kinds of sentences. *If-then*s and *either-or*s tended to surface in much more casual settings. Historical texts from Herodotus and from the book of Judges in the Bible display clusters of them in direct speech, flowing from agents' intentions, and frequently taking the form of threats or promises:

If you do not provide for your own interests, yet we must not overlook this, that the race of Eurysthenes should become extinct. Do you therefore put away the wife whom you have, since she bears no children, and marry another; and by so doing you will gratify the Spartans. (Herodotus)

As we see you strongly attached to the wife whom you have, act as follows, and do not oppose it, *lest* the Spartans should come to some unusual resolution respecting you. (Herodotus)

If thou wilt give the Ammonites into my hand, then whoever comes forth from the doors of my house to meet me, when I return victorious from the Ammonites, shall be the LORD's, and I will offer him up for a burnt offering. (Judges)

My father, *if* you have opened your mouth to the LORD, do to me according to what has gone forth from your mouth, now that the LORD has avenged you on your enemies, on the Ammonites. (Judges)[1]

Speakers use *if-then*s and *either-or*s regularly to persuade and dis-courage – to influence human behaviour in particular situations. When civil authorities promulgated them as general universals to apply to everybody, they gave them the form of law: if anyone violates the law, he or she will receive punishment; unless people's actions conform to the law, they will not benefit; one either obeys the law or becomes an outlaw.

All such laws derive ultimately from the will of the legislator or speaker. It is that will which determines whether the relation con-necting antecedent and consequent does follow necessarily or the disjuncts are in fact exhaustive. Implementation depends on the con-tingencies of legal procedures, of historical circumstance, or of human commitments. The language suggests necessity and exhaus-tiveness, but experience shows that the consequences can be avoided. Human will is notoriously inconstant: trustworthy and faithful judges, while frequent enough, do not appear everywhere and in all circum-stances; politicians dissemble, making promises they know they can-not keep; in the face of resistance, people can avert threatened punishments; mercy may temper justice; and crowds as well as indi-viduals can be fickle, creating havoc where they promise order.

Because the link between conditional and result, or between the set of disjuncts, depended on the contingency of human intentions, Aristotle did not use conditionals and disjunctions for the systematic investigation of nature. Any thing or event is the result of at least four contributing conditions: its material; its principle or form of organi-zation; the trigger that brings its material and its form together; and its function. Were any of these to be changed, the event would not take place; so there is no necessary connection from any one of them to the effect. For Aristotle, the rigour of science involves classifying the form of things, their types and species. Individual things might vary from the standard because of variations in material conditions

---

1 The quotations are from Herodotus, *History*, trans. H. Cary (London: G. Bell, 1885), V, §§39, 40, and Judges 11: 29–40 (RSV).

or the effectiveness of the agent; none the less we can understand their nature in terms of what they in principle are to be. This is why Aristotle adopts predication and syllogisms as the basis for logical (and scientific) reasoning.

It is the Stoics who develop the logic of conditionals and disjuncts. And they can do so because they transfer their application from the world of human affairs to the world of nature. They understand the functioning of nature in a new way by shifting the focus from entities with their predicated qualities to events, whose regularity suggests an analogy to human society. Like the conventions of the social order, natural processes follow repeated patterns; this implies that they too result from will and design; both are the work of lawmakers.

A comment of Cicero's makes this clear:

Nothing is more impressive than the governance of the cosmos; therefore it is governed by the rational planning of the gods ... [Further,] since there are gods (if they really exist, as they certainly do) it is necessary that they be alive, and not only alive but also rational and bound to each other by a kind of political bond and society, governing this single cosmos like some shared republic or city. It follows that they possess the same kind of reason as is present in mankind, that the same truth is found in both [gods and men] and the same law, which consists in injunctions to do what is right and avoid what is wrong.[2]

In other words, laws govern nature in the same way that conditionals govern human society. We can describe its regularities using those *if-thens* and *either-or*s that people had previously used to organize the political arena and govern human interaction.

---

2 Cicero, *On the Nature of the Gods*, 2: §§ 76, 78, 79. Cf. Cleanthes' *The Hymn to Zeus*: "Zeus, leader of nature, guiding everything with law." These citations are from *Hellenistic Philosophy: Introductory Readings*, trans. B. Inwood and L.P. Gerson (Indianapolis: Hackett, 1988), 111, 102. In a similar vein, Diogenes Laertius, in giving his account of the Stoics, says: "The cosmos is administered by mind and providence (as Chrysippus says in book five of his *On Providence* and Posidonius in book thirteen of his *On Gods*), since mind penetrates every part of it just as soul does us." Again he writes: "Sometimes they explain 'nature' as that which holds the cosmos together, and other times as that which makes things on earth grow ... They say that this [i.e., nature] aims at both the advantageous and at pleasure, as is clear from the craftsmanlike [structure or activity] of man ... Fate is a continuous string of causes of things which exist, or a rational principle according to which the cosmos is managed." Diogenes Laertius, 7. 138, 148, 149, in ibid., 97, 99, 100.

Thus the Stoics introduce this understanding of the lawlike governance of nature; by drawing an analogy with the sphere of politics,
they generate the conception of natural law. For them, the laws of
nature resemble human laws in that they are universal conditionals
which are the result of rational decision and a kind of political determination. Nature too has injunctions to do what is right and avoid
what is wrong. But in drawing this analogy, they add a further wrin-
kle. The Stoics' gods, unlike humans, are completely trustworthy;
each sequence of events follows necessarily, not affected by contingencies; disjunctive alternatives can be exhaustively enumerated. So
the laws of nature are absolutely reliable. For this reason, the Stoics
could confidently apply conditionals and disjunctions in their investigation of the nature of things. These sentence forms articulate the
unalterable laws that the gods set down. By drawing inferences from
conditionals, one can predict the course of nature. Because conditionals and disjunctions have become comprehensive – as reliable in
nature as they may be in thought – Stoic cosmology can exploit the
valid logical forms of *modus ponens, modus tollens,* and hypothetical
and disjunctive syllogisms.[3]

The Stoics thereby transform the understanding of the world. In
the Greek myths, gods can be as fickle as humans. In Hebrew narra-
tives, God can regret a promise, or withdraw a threat. Aristotle's appeal to forms allows for variations from the norm. Nature and history
are rife with contingency. The Stoics, however, hold that the gods are
not only rational, but also absolutely trustworthy and faithful, ensuring that things always happen as they have ordained. So one can investigate nature to determine not simply why things are the way they
are, but why things happen in the order they do, and why only certain
possibilities follow from particular circumstances. The language of
universal conditionals and disjunctions introduces a transition from
nature as a hierarchy of entities to nature as a regulated sequence of
events and processes.

Christianity found the Stoic conception of a trustworthy and reliable
deity congenial to its understanding of God as lawgiver and judge.
So, throughout the Middle Ages the use of conditionals and

---

3 Compare Diogenes Laertius, 7. 71–83, in ibid., 86–9.

disjunctions expanded. Once the phrase "natural law" came to apply not only to the moral realm, but also in the world of nature, however, it began to develop a sense of its own; and the link to will and intention atrophied and died. As the original analogy disappeared from view, the laws of nature became nothing but necessary and exhaustive regularities simply inherent in the nature of things. As scientists discovered more and more such patterns, they no longer derived them from the will of God, but concluded that the necessities of nature bound even God himself. In due course, any appeal to the divine became redundant.

Once the appeal to will and intention disappears from the use of conditionals and disjunctions, they lose the intuitive ground for their necessity. The justification for their reliability derives not from general principles, but from the manner of their application to the world of nature and society. They need to satisfy the test for comprehensiveness.

What now becomes critical is finding which sequences in nature are necessary and which sets of alternatives are exhaustive. Here as well, Mill's methods have a role to play. Experiments control variables, altering only the condition in question, and it is to have the same effects, no matter what the circumstances; when the consequent is absent, the condition is missing as well. Initially in the sphere of mechanics, scientists isolated processes from interfering circumstances and discovered a number of specific regularities. If theories suggested two alternative explanations, scientists designed experiments in which the two disjuncts would produce quite diverse consequences, so that the result determines which set of conditionals are in fact most likely to be comprehensive and objective. As their ability to control experiments increased, scientists achieved impressive results in physics, chemistry, medicine, and an increasing number of other disciplines.

When one moves outside the laboratory, however, it is harder to isolate a particular sequence. When one conducts a sociological survey, one needs to ensure that the sample is representative of the total population. But the conclusions are reliable only within a margin of error. Even in mechanics, when one adopts a model where more than two bodies act on each other, it is not easy to generate clear conditionals and laws. Once we move to biology and the life sciences, matters become even more complicated in at least two ways. First, a stimulus

can evoke a response, but that response in its turn can have an effect
on the original stimulant, creating a reciprocal dynamic. In this way,
an alien bacterium introduced into a primitive form of cell develops a
symbiotic relation with it to produce a new kind of complexity;[4] and a
fungus interacts with algae to produce lichens. Second, a virus may be
necessary to generate a disease, but that result is not assured, since it
depends on a number of other suitable conditions – in the recipient
organism, in the environment, in the way it is introduced. There is no
necessary causal sequence from presence of virus to disease. It is almost as if we have to reintroduce the variety of conditions that Aristotle
identified: original material base, initiating cause, formal capacity of
the recipient, and so on. Instead of relying on the universality and
strict regularity that the conditional requires, one cites probabilities
and likelihoods. Indeed, quantum mechanics has concluded that
even in physics one cannot always establish strict necessity.

To retain the comprehensive objectivity of conditional statements,
logicians have fallen back on the distinction between a sufficient and
a necessary condition. A sufficient condition is one in which, once it
occurs, the consequent must follow. Where such regularities happen
without fail, we have a strict natural law. Whenever the moon's orbit
brings it exactly opposite the sun with the earth in between, for example, we have a lunar eclipse.

When we think about events as they actually happen in the natural
and social world, however, we realize that things are seldom that simple. An event occurs because a number of conditions conspire to
come together at a particular instant and in a particular place. The
lightning had to strike at 10:45 on that Friday evening, and at the rise
on the road where it turns towards the town, for the maple tree to
have fallen directly on the passing Ford. The car had to be going at
just 83 kilometres per hour; the journey had to begin at just 10:12;
the wind had to be blowing from the north-west at 50 kilometres
per hour ...

One can easily multiply the number of conditions that had to
conspire for the result to happen in just the way it did. Had any one
of them been different, the accident would not have occurred.
When we think about such events, we find no one-to-one connection

4 See Fortey, *Life*, 61.

between any single prior condition and the final result. To fathom the full cause of the resulting event, we have to include all the contributing circumstances, which could easily have happened otherwise, or combined in different ways. It would seem to be a matter of pure contingency that all these conditions came together in just this way at just this particular moment and location.

So we turn instead from sufficient conditions to necessary conditions. In this case, if an event happens, then we use Mill's methods to see if there is some event among its prior conditions that had to be present for it to emerge in the way it does. We start from the result and conclude to the condition. Now, it is the antecedent of the *if-then* that happens later; and the consequent refers to an event that precedes it. The sequence of conditioning is the opposite of the sequence in time. So whenever in the earlier paragraph I introduce the phrase "had to," I am identifying a necessary condition. *If* the accident happened as it did, *then* the lightning bolt must have occurred at 10:45. In this case, as I said, one cannot find regular sequences from before to after. But we do find a lawlike pattern when working from after to before. While the presence of the malaria parasite is not a sufficient condition for developing the disease, since many people may carry the bacterium without ever contracting it, it is none the less a universal necessary condition: *if* anyone develops the fever, *then* the malaria parasite must have been present. So laws that use conditional judgments to identify necessary conditions reverse the temporal order. The antecedent happened later, and the consequent earlier.[5]

There are many events, however, in which one can identify neither a universally valid sufficient condition nor any necessary conditions. When we turn to the historical arena, for example, we may find that a multitude of contributing factors led to a declaration of war, none of which would have been sufficient on its own, and indeed, none of which is necessary, since, were any missing, other factors could have conspired to the same result. Here we have conditions that are

---

5 For a strict determinism, which requires a forward-moving necessity, the fact that we often have to move from sufficient to necessary conditions is inconvenient, since it is much harder to prove that a multitude of independent, diverse conditions had no other option than to come together at this particular time and in this particular place. To assume that there must be such a necessary forward direction simply begs the question.

neither necessary nor sufficient, but which together contribute to bringing about the awful consequence. At this point, any attempt to appeal to the necessary conditionals of law fails, and what remains is an analysis of causes that identifies a number of contributing and interacting conditions ranging far beyond Aristotle's four: time and place being the most general; reciprocal interaction between different agents whose actions and reactions mutually stimulate a developing escalation of sentiment; the particular weather conditions at the time; the interference of other parties; a purely chance encounter; and so on. The ideal of a set of isolated and singular sequences is completely unattainable.

The universal reliability the Stoics identified as essential to applying conditionals and disjunctions comprehensively has found validation in those spheres of science and society where we can identify either sufficient or necessary conditions. Their argument forms have even retained a measure of plausibility in spheres of investigation that have had to fall back on a probability calculus – where there can never be firm predictions, but only estimates of likely results. But it becomes much more risky in spheres of complex interaction – in particular, where events result from the deliberate and willed actions of many diverse human agents that reciprocally influence one another. Here, contingencies are endemic, and necessary connections are few and far between. In these situations, we find ourselves once again with a lack of strict reliability, much as happened before the Stoics drew their analogy between human society and nature.

We now come back to our central question: what light does the exhaustive necessity implicit in conditionals and disjunctions throw on our investigation of the tendrils of thought? Our discussion of dilemmas suggests that tendrils of meaning may justify some forms of *if-then* or *either-or*. In the case of human laws, it is the will and authority of the legislator that maintain the connection. But in the world of nature, we must rely on the disciplined observation of experience. Necessity means that the antecedent never occurs where the consequent does not apply. While we can never draw such a conclusion with absolute necessity, since the future is always open, we can reduce contingencies by varying attendant circumstances as we try to exhaust the range of possible alternatives. The success of these controlled experiments has produced a large number of regularities that have proven to be reliable in practice. We integrate them into the way we interact with the world, and, as necessary conditions, they become so familiar that they form part of our definitions and expectations. In other words, many of the tendrils that we follow as we draw implications stem from our disciplined interaction with the world – from organizing our experience using conditionals and disjunctions. Their basic sense of necessity and exhaustiveness combines with the concrete content of experienced life in all its dimensions to produce tendrils that link to a wide range of other meanings and terms.

These natural links of conditioning and viable options are the source of many tendrils of meaning. So tendrils do not derive simply from definitions, but also emerge through disciplined investigation of the way the world is. The concepts we use are not just organized in a hierarchy of genus and species, but have many other links and connections that have emerged from human interaction with the world of nature and history. The network of tendrils is continually expanding as knowledge of the world develops.

14

Arguments from Analogy

IN TEXTBOOKS ON LOGIC, arguments from analogy are the poor cousins. They do not provide the strict necessity that occurs in syllogisms or *modus ponens*; there are no methods to ensure reliability as exist for inductive generalizations; they frequently lead people astray. Yet they are in wide use, even by the people who worry most about logical rigour; they turn out to be indispensable for establishing the plausibility of claims.

One of Francis Bacon's arguments for an empirical science, for example, goes like this: "The human understanding is like a false mirror, which, receiving rays irregularly, distorts and discolours the nature of the things by mingling its own nature with them."[1] While acknowledging that our thinking and a mirror are radically different, he none the less identifies the way receiving, mingling, and distorting interact in both contexts. Implicit is the conclusion he wants to justify: it is the receiving and mingling, common to both, that produce the distortion in our understanding.

Even Frege is not immune to such appeals:

The following analogy will perhaps clarify these relationships [linking reference, conceptual meaning, and ideas]. Someone observes the Moon through a telescope. I compare the Moon itself to the *Bedeutung* [reference]; it is the object of the observation, mediated by the real image projected by the object glass in the interior of the telescope, and by the retinal image of the observer. The former I compare to the sense, the latter is like the idea [*Vorstellung*] or intuition [*Anschauung*] ... This analogy might be developed still further,

---

1 Francis Bacon, *Novum Organum* (Chicago: Open Court, 1994), Aphorism 41.

by assuming A's retinal image made visible to B; or A might see his own retinal image in a mirror. In this way we might perhaps show how an idea can itself be taken as an object, but as such is not for the observer what it is for the person having the idea.[2]

Since the object of reference (*Bedeuting*), its conceptual meaning or sense (*Sinn*), and our idea (*Vorstellung*) of it relate in the same way as moon, real image, and retinal image when someone looks through a telescope, Frege concludes that, just as we cannot have anyone else's retinal image (even though it might become an object for investigation), so we cannot have other people's ideas.

The frequent use of analogical arguments to justify or make plausible a claim seems paradoxical, when one considers their reputation. Yet they are valuable precisely because more formal inferences do not lead us very far and seldom, if ever, take us into new ground. A syllogism simply spells out the results of our definitions, however they have been formulated. It may make us aware of implications we did not previously notice, but it does not lead to new insights. Conditional and disjunctive inferences start from universal and necessary relations, but these are justified by other means. In contrast, an argument from analogy uses a familiar relationship to illuminate and elaborate one that is more obscure.

There is another advantage to this argument form, which few commentators notice. Syllogisms are constructs of predications, in which the copula or verb simply brings the subject under the predicate or excludes the one from the other. The components of *if-then*s and *either-or*s are whole sentences, of whatever sort. Neither logical system considers sentences centred around a transitive or intransitive verb – where verbs integrate a number of diverse units into a complex structure. An argument from analogy, however, takes as its premise a network of familiar relations and applies this network to another, more questionable complex. This makes it particularly suitable for drawing inferences from complex verbal sentences. The examples I cite above, for example, compare neither the qualifications of a subject nor the links between propositions, but the *dynamic* of reflecting, in the Bacon example, and the *activity* of observing, in Frege's. The

2 G. Frege, "On *Sinn* and *Bedeutung*" [30], in *Frege Reader*, ed. Beaney, 155.

centre of attention is most appropriately a verb – a verb that provides the inferential link to the conclusion.

None of the standard forms of traditional logic, whether Aristotelian or symbolic, does justice to this kind of sentence. To be sure, a predicate concept can include verbs, but subordinates them to some more static noun or pronoun.[3] And functional analysis introduces relations that connect a number of terms, but the relational function simply couples its terms together in the same way predicates link with subjects.[4] Because traditional logic has ignored the critical role verbs play, many of the specific tendrils that make an inference from analogy so productive have dropped from view.

Arguments from analogy then are able to build from specific relationships that reach out from a central verb. We regularly use verbs to integrate a number of distinct functions into a single sentence:

To fulfil his promise, John at the garden party yesterday gave a copy of the book he had written to the chief librarian of the library that had hosted its launch so that the collection of his works would be complete.

In this example, the simple verb "gave" unites into one complex construction the donor, the rationale, the location, the time, the gift, the recipient, and the expected consequences. To complicate things further, subordinate clauses qualify two elements (the gift and the recipient) and introduce secondary connections to other parts of the sentence. Translating such a sentence into a simple predication or the symbols of formal logic would dissolve that network into an abstract and indefinite collection. And it would be of little use in seeing how this complex relates to some other, such as:

To satisfy its hunger, the chimpanzee in the demonstration last week handed over the stick he had broken off to the keeper of the zoo where he lives so that a coconut could be retrieved from a nearby tree.

---

3 In Aristotelian logic, "mirrors *reflect* images" becomes "mirrors are things *that reflect* images."

4 The symbols of formal logic cannot distinguish, for example, between the dynamic network created by a verb and the more static relations of "greater than," "between," and "double." And it tends to incorporate the language of function to the language of concepts and nouns – of a thought with rigid definition and retained significance. Verbs, as we see below, because of multiple inflections and the dynamic links that reach out to an indefinite range of actions and entities, are more plastic.

The specific network of relations that makes the analogy so useful in exploring chimpanzee psychology would evaporate.

When we look at how philosophers have used arguments from analogy, we regularly find that it is a specified *activity* that makes the inference plausible. A major practitioner of this kind of reasoning was Plato. Consider a typical passage from the first book of the *Republic* (342^{d-e}), where Socrates chats with Thrasymachus:

"We agreed that a doctor in the precise sense is a ruler of bodies, not a money-maker. Wasn't that agreed?"

"Yes."

"So a ship's captain in the precise sense is a ruler of sailors, not a sailor?"

"That's what we agreed."

"Doesn't it follow that a ship's captain or ruler won't seek and order what is advantageous to himself, but what is advantageous to a sailor?"

He reluctantly agreed.

"So, then, Thrasymachus, no one in a position of rule, insofar as he is a ruler, seeks or orders what is advantageous to himself, but what is advantageous to his subjects."[5]

Thrasymachus had advanced the definition of justice as nothing other than the advantage of the stronger. In reply, Socrates suggests that, since the exercise of justice requires an expertise in governing, one can learn something about it by drawing analogies with other crafts such as medicine, navigation, and horse breeding, where one must also act with skill in deciding what other beings are to do. In all these cases, practitioners (doctor, captain, or breeder, respectively) perform actions that have an effect on ill bodies, sailors, or horses; and they exercise the craft appropriately when they do so not for their own benefit, but for the recipient's. There is a network of relations that these activities share, for all that healing, sailing, and animal husbandry are quite different from each other – a network that, Socrates suggests, is a kind of "ruling." That network Socrates wants to extend to a ruler in the proper sense. The verb "rule" serves as a nexus linking a variety of functions; and that specific nexus establishes the strength of the inference.

5 Trans. G.W.A. Grube, rev. C.D.C. Reeve, in *Plato: Complete Works*, ed. J.M. Cooper (Indianapolis: Hackett, 1997), 987.

This kind of reasoning is not unique to Plato:

Mencius said to King Hsüan of Ch'i, "Supposing one of your ministers had gone on a journey to Ch'u, leaving his wife and children with a friend, and upon returning found his family starving, what do you think he should do?"

The King said, "He should cut off all relations with that friend."

Mencius said, "Suppose now that the Leader of the Knights had no control over the knights, then what would you do?"

The King said, "I should dismiss him."

Mencius said, "Suppose now the kingdom to be ill-governed, what then should be done?"

The King turned to his courtiers and spoke of other things.[6]

In Mencius's analogy, persons responsible for the well-being and good order of the people under them are judged on the basis of how they behave or treat their wards. It then applies this relational structure to the role of a king. The argument works because it, once again, draws on the multiple relations involved in exercising responsibility. When one has the task of looking after a community, one ensures the health of the people in one's charge and maintains order and discipline.

In a discussion in chapter 8 above, we learned from Kant that judgments integrate a number of components into a single, complex thought. He limits his analysis to the traditional categorical, conditional, and disjunctive forms. But once we take into account sentences where a verb is the central concept, we come on more complicated kinds of connections. Each active verb contains implicit links that require and allow a number of other features to complete its sense. So these judgment forms make a valuable contribution not only to analogical reasoning but also to our investigation of how tendrils reach out from concepts to connect with each other more generally. By comparing familiar processes and actions, we find clues that explain how, in a less obvious setting, a diverse range of features and characteristics may be integrated into a relatively coherent pattern. It is not surprising that arguments from analogy play a key role in the formation of explanatory hypotheses.

6 Mencius, tr. W. Dobson (Toronto: University of Toronto Press, 1963) 1.12, page 18.

Thus arguments from analogy are able to exploit judgments integrated by a transitive or intransitive verb. At the same time, this is the only kind of argument we have for drawing inferences from what I call "verbal sentences." Working with the tendrils that reach out from a central concept, they show how such interconnections may be effective in related spheres. But this critical concept is no longer a noun, identifying a particular kind of thing, as in predication. Nor is it a conditional or disjunctive connection. It is a verb, dynamic and active, naming a process.

And it is not the specific content of the verbs that is important for the inference, but the way they invite and require a complex of related terms. Discussion of concepts and ideas has tended to use nouns almost exclusively as examples; and this has directed our attention to things, named by thoughts that are atomic and fixed. But verbs articulate meaning no less than nouns; and these meanings are not independent of their context. While each has a distinctive definition, this is not a fixed and isolated sense, but a dynamic one that incorporates a variety of tendrils reaching out towards other terms, requiring some to complete its meaning and allowing for others to render more precise its specific application. There is always a related subject; there is often an object; and indirect objects, subordinate clauses, and adverbs may further flesh it out. The verb conceptually integrates all of these many components into a single, complex judgment.

By broadening our understanding of concepts to include verbs, with all their dynamic implications, we introduce a broader perspective on the tendrils that bind conceptual constructions together. And it is just the way these tendrils work that arguments from analogy exploit when they move between related, but distinctive verbs.

The primary verb in any sentence does not have a fixed form, but the speaker or writer can inflect it in at least six ways, each of which identifies a possible link to other terms. All finite verbs can be inflected to indicate mood, tense, aspect, voice, number, and person.

First, the form, or *mood*, of a verb spells out the way the conceptual content of the sentence as a whole relates to reality, suggesting its potential comprehensiveness. Mood differentiates among a number of such relations. Logicians rely on the indicative mood, which asserts that the expression agrees or disagrees with the facts. But other moods are equally important: the imperative demands agreement;

the interrogative asks whether the agreement holds; the subjunctive refers to the uncertainty of the future, while the optative expresses a wish or an exhortation, and conditional sentences can use both to express contrary-to-fact possibility.[7]

Second, through *tense*, verbs make precise the time in which an action takes place: not simply whether it is past, present, or future, but also how one action is before (or after) another through such forms as the future perfect or pluperfect. Tense situates the action in some time in general and invites a linking adverbial phrase that would render it more specific.

Third, through *aspect*, verbs indicate whether an action is complete or is continuing. While aspect does not surface in most Western grammars, it remains in the contrast between the imperfect and the preterit or simple past ("was finishing," "finished"), or between the perfect and the pluperfect ("has written," "had written"). Ancient Hebrew structured verbs by aspect rather than by tense. And English follows the same pattern with inflected verbs: with "goes" or "have" (incomplete) and "went" or "had" (completed) being the key finite inflections of the verbs "to go" and "to have"; all other forms use participles or infinitives with an auxiliary.[8]

These three functions of the verb – mood, tense, and aspect – all specify how the conceptual content of a sentence relates to the real world. They do not directly affect the way terms relate among themselves. For this, we turn to three more functions.

Fourth, as Aristotle's final four categories suggest,[9] finite verbs can indicate *voice* – whether an action is performed by the subject of the

---

7 I base this list on the forms of Greek grammar. Other languages may offer further alternatives.

8 In grammar, a "finite" verb is one that is limited by number and person. Tenses other than the present or past use participles ("gone" or "going") or the infinitive ("go") with a finite auxiliary: "*will* go," "*was* going," "*has* gone." The one other distinctive form – the subjunctive ("if it *be* true"; "it is necessary that he *be* corrected") – has now almost completely disappeared from everyday use. By Hellenistic times, Hebrew had adjusted the use of its forms to express tense rather than aspect: the indefinite aspect became the future, the definite the past, and the participle the present. This practice has continued in the contemporary language.

9 Aristotle's examples for these final four are all finite verbs in the third person singular: being-in-a-position ("is-lying"), having ("has-shoes-on"), doing ("cuts"), and being-affected ("is cut"). Aristotle, *Categories*, 1^{b}25–2^{a}4. I use J.L. Ackrill's names for the categories but correct his last two examples to reflect the original's use of a finite verb. See *The Complete Works of Aristotle*, ed. Jonathan Barnes (Princeton, NJ: Princeton

sentence (active), is done to the subject(passive), or is habitual (middle). English tends to have only the active and passive voices, but traces of the ancient middle remain in the reflexive verbs of German and French.[10] Unlike tense or mood, voice does influence the way the various concepts or thoughts relate to each other. As Aristotle suggested, it can indicate activity, receptivity or, in the middle voice, a transient stance or a more permanent state.[11]

Finally, many languages inflect a finite verb to indicate *number* – whether the agent is one, two, or many – and *person* – whether it includes the speaker, the person spoken to, or someone else.

These determinations then define more precisely the relations that bind verbs to other components of the sentence as well as to the world around us. All have an explicit or implicit subject; transitive verbs require an object; some point towards an indirect object. Thus "gave," as we saw in our example above, requires a donor, a recipient, and a gift. But the verb also contains tendrils that the user can flesh out with supplementary information, not only the time that the tense suggests, but also place, purpose, means, manner, circumstance, and contributing condition. Finally, as in our example, the connection between the donor, the gift, and the library may become more precise by indicating that the donor wrote the book and the library hosted its launch. In a verbal sentence, then, a number of tendrils reach out from its central dynamic concept.

English articulates many of these tendrils through prepositions and conjunctions, while other languages do so by the way they inflect the

University Press, 1984), I, 4. Émile Benveniste (see next note) perceptively notes that the examples for these categories represent four distinct Greek verb forms: the present middle (where the recipient of the action is the same as the subject), the perfect middle, the present active, and the present passive.

10 Émile Benveniste, "Actif et moyen dans le verbe," in *Problèmes de linguistique générale*, 2 vols. (Paris: Gallimard, 1966, 1974), 1, 168–75, postulates that the middle voice antedated the passive, at least in the Indo-European languages. Its absence from English should not mislead us into ignoring its significance.

11 There are other forms of verbal inflection that can lead further afield. Ancient Hebrew, once again, has intensive and causative forms: for example "hit," "batter," and "cause to hit." It was the range of verbal inflections in the Hopi language that encouraged Benjamin Whorf to develop his hypothesis that language influences thought. See Benjamin Lee Whorf, *Language, Thought and Reality*, ed. John B. Carroll (Cambridge, Mass.: MIT Press, 1956), especially 51ff. and 112ff.

other components. Most obvious, adjectives qualify nouns, adverbs qualify verbs as well as adjectives, and each usually has a distinctive shape. As well, the tendrils that connect nouns, participles, and clauses to the central verb are not left implicit but made explicit by altering the beginning, ending, or constituent vowels of a term to indicate case: *nominative* (or subjective) for the agent; *accusative* (or objective) for the recipient; *dative* for the beneficiary; *instrumental* for the means; *genitive* for that which qualifies another noun; *locative* for place; and *vocative* for person spoken to. Over time, each of these cases may develop more subtle and complicated meanings, so that it can indicate a variety of connections.

Cases thus provide nouns with explicit tendrils that show how they relate to the central verb as well as to each other. By applying these inflections to adjectives, participles, and subordinate conjunctions, the speaker can extend links to clauses and phrases that have their own inflected verbs, producing a highly complex network in which tendrils connect a number of concepts, both static and dynamic, into a single, richly articulated, temporally ordered, yet coherent sentence. Classical Greek, Latin, and German are languages in our Western tradition that embody this kind of explicit linkage in their syntax.

Not all the tendrils of a verbal nexus become evident in the syntax of a language. Inflections are rare in English, yet, as we saw above with the example of "gave," the central verb can have all kinds of links with other thoughts. Most of these are implicit in the basic integrating concept. A verb's definition includes the key conjuncts it requires to be complete; its inflections open up links to time, place, conditions, and circumstances. Once we add prepositional phrases and subordinate conjunctions, we have a rich diversity of tendrils that bind the various components of a verbal sentence into a conceptual totality. In other words, there are far more tendrils of thought than simply the relation of genus and species, as in universal predication, or necessary connection, as in conditionals and disjunctions.

Apart from my brief reference to mood, we have not talked about how the complex concepts expressed in a verbal nexus can comprehend the world. For descriptions of events, which are primarily a function of ideas, there is no great problem, for one refers either to direct experience or to reliable sources. But where a verbal nexus integrates pure concepts, as in an explanation, it is not so easy to establish its objective force. Whenever we try to make sense of a particular event – why it happens in the way it does – we are looking not for the particular circumstances when it occurred, but for conceptual tendrils that link the various features together in a credible way.

We are helped in this quest by drawing analogies with other processes that have a similar concatenation of factors; the analogy with selective breeding, for example, led Darwin towards the hypothesis of evolution by natural selection. Explanatory proposals need to be plausible, in the sense that they draw on tendrils already familiar from careful experiment and disciplined observation. But that does not make them reliable and trustworthy. There may be a wide range of analogies that seem appropriate; and there is no obvious way of deciding among them, since all may well take account of the facts. Full comprehensiveness does not come easily to conceptual explanations.[12]

There is no direct way of comparing explanations with experience, for what distinguishes them is not events that in fact occur, but the way we suppose their general characteristics link together. What we do instead is draw out implications from competing hypotheses. We explore their implicit tendrils, looking for kinds of events that would fit with each of the options – until we come to some that are incompatible: what one would lead us to expect, the other would exclude. We create an exclusive disjunction. Then we try to set up a controlled experiment (better, a set of them) through which we can see which of the options actually does occur. We reject the hypothesis that fails, since the successful one is more comprehensive.

The classic illustration of this process involved deciding between the Newtonian worldview and Einstein's theory of general relativity. In the solar eclipse of 1919, the sun would have blocked light from a distant star had Newton's view of space been correct, but not, if Einstein's was. Astronomers observed the star at the critical moment. Experience helped to decide between the two explanations, but

---

12 Darwin's specific explanation of how new species evolve has not stood the test of time, as careful observation and experimentation has revealed very complex relationships among features both evident and recessive, as well as between strings of DNA and their triggering and inhibiting conditions.

conceptual thought carefully constructed this experience, building
on the tendrils implicit in the two alternatives.[13]

Such tests are sufficient to prove the inadequacy of any conceptual
explanation that fails; but they do not establish definitively its alternatives. The latter too may have limitations that lie outside the critical
experiment. They continue to be falsifiable. Anomalies might appear
in the future that trigger a search for more encompassing and inclusive hypotheses; critical tests may reveal their success and the failure
of Einstein's model. And such possibilities will continue to emerge,
closing off any definitive resolution. In any case of a general verbal
nexus – an explanation – full comprehensiveness is never realizable.
We must continue to be humble in adopting even our most sophisticated conceptual explanations about the nature of things.

Arguments from analogy have introduced us to a large range of conceptual tendrils, some of which are explicit in inflections of verbs and
nouns, others of which are implicit in the meaning of the basic actions. While it is impossible to make the resulting concepts fully comprehensive in those cases where the verbal nexus is general rather
than specific, these networks can be productive and significant.
Analogies may suggest links we have not yet noticed and suggest
possibilities not present in our direct experience. By exploring such
tenuous and implicit tendrils, conceptual thinking may open up
alternative interconnections that both experts and other observers
routinely ignore because of the immediate concerns of contemporary existence and the inclination to presume that we have an answer for all questions. Analogy and verbal nexus provide a setting by
which we can expand and transform our conceptual world.

Such explorations draw on habits of mind that have freed themselves from reliance on ideas and are able to reflect on nothing else
but concepts and their explicit and implicit tendrils. Since the languages we use have nurtured and structured many of those habits,
the kinds of tendrils we explore may well reflect the particular syntactical practices of our native speech. I noted above the considerable

---

13 In their calculations for an earlier eclipse, researchers made some mistakes
which would not have exposed the difference. However. the first world war prevented
them making any controlled observations.

difference between highly inflected languages such as ancient Greek and German and the simpler structure of English. It is worth our while to turn aside and consider in the next chapter the way syntax influences the kinds of explanations various cultures advance. There may be more variety in the range of conceptual tendrils than we might expect.

15

Linguistic Variations

IN OUR DISCUSSION OF LANGUAGE IN CHAPTER 4, we took no notice of words' relationships with each other. Arguments from analogy, however, have introduced us to the way tendrils reach out from a central verb to the other components of a sentence. These connections, whether with nouns, adverbs, clauses, or phrases, create a network of interrelations. So it is not only the basic meaning of our terms that needs refining if we are to communicate effectively with our fellows, but also the way they link together into a meaningful complex. If we heard only a sequence of sounds, each with its independent meaning, it would mean little. The spoken sentence requires other signs to tell us how those meanings intersect and complement each other. To manipulate a language, we require not only a vocabulary, but also a good sense of the syntactical conventions; for syntax gives us "the grammatical arrangement of words in speech and writing to show their connection and relation."[1] Though standard in courses teaching second languages, these conventions are seldom taught explicitly to native speakers. Through the interaction of success and failure, agreement and disagreement over time, we develop language competence. These conventions become crystallized and fixed in our common practice because they are a crucial means of avoiding ambiguity. When we hear a spoken sentence, we make sense of it only because we expect the speaker to use those conventions with care and precision. Misunderstandings happen because

---

1 *Oxford Concise Dictionary*, 7th ed. (Oxford: Clarendon, 1982), 1084.

speakers have not used them correctly, simply disregard them, or invoke terms with several meanings.

Syntactical rules enable us to link words to each other. And they do so by means of signs – sounds and letters that point not to a meaning derived from our experience, but to types of relationship. Languages, however, vary in the strategies they adopt to avoid syntactical ambiguity. Some adjoin distinctive sounds or syllables before or after nouns and verbs to modify their sense. We have reviewed six ways – mood, tense, aspect, voice, number, and person – whereby we can inflect verbs to indicate how they are to integrate the components of a sentence with the context in which it is spoken. Nouns as well can be inflected; case indicates a noun's connection to its immediate verb and other nouns;[2] gender allows use of inflected pronouns and adjectives to distinguish among various terms in a discussion without too much ambiguity;[3] and number indicates how many items: one, two, or several. Some languages mesh words together into complex signs that incorporate a number of interrelated meanings, some more like nouns and some more like verbs. Still others do not inflect the basic terms, but introduce particles – prepositions, conjunctions, and place markers – which tell listeners how to link verbs and nouns into a coherent pattern. Almost all rely on conventions about how to string words into an ordered sequence of before and after.

So syntax is critical to our use of language. When we want to communicate a complex thought to our fellows, we not only break it up into a number of discrete nouns, adjectives, verbs, and adverbs, but also provide clues to the way they are to be reconnected; and when we hear or read a complex utterance, we rely on those clues to fit them together into a single, meaningful sentence. In conversation we are constantly using such clues – the syntactical devices of our language – to analyse and synthesize our thoughts. Skill in this linguistic process of analysis and synthesis develops early and soon becomes

2 The languages we consider have the nominative, accusative, genitive, and dative cases; other languages may have ablative, vocative, locative, and so on.

3 While masculine and feminine may have started out as a way of distinguishing among animals, they have often been extended to a wide range of inanimate and abstract terms. In addition, one can have a neuter gender or discriminate by gender between human, living, inanimate, and abstract terms.

second nature as people become adept in articulating thoughts into coherent wholes. As links between terms, syntactical conventions function in ways that resemble the role of the tendrils of meaning we identified above. How are the two related?

Tendrils emerge from the core meaning of a term – from the nature of its definition, from the necessary connections we have discovered through our experience. They are specific. Syntactical conventions are general and formal, they can be applied in a number of contexts, and, when we confront a new situation that does not fit easily with our rules, we adapt our rules accordingly. At times, we use them to discriminate among a number of possible links associated with a particular tendril. At other times, they are so general that we refer back to our sense of the terms used to figure out what is involved.

There is, however, one scenario in which syntactical conventions may mould and suggest possible tendrils. When we are looking for an explanation of something that has happened, or when we face a puzzle and are trying to discover a solution, we are in effect casting around for possible links that may be significant, yet have been either overlooked or not yet created. We have before us a number of components: things that have happened both familiar and unexpected, earlier explanations, and unrelated experiences and thoughts; and we are looking for a way through them – a way to fit them together into a coherent pattern. At this point, we may well appeal for guidance to the formal types of links that syntactical conventions enshrine. As we saw above, they became second nature as we acquired language competence. In other words, syntax may suggest tendrils not previously noticed.

Conclusive proof of such a hypothesis is not easy to establish. Controlled experiments would be difficult if not impossible to design. However, we can illustrate its plausibility by comparing the syntactical conventions that distinguish languages from each other with explanations provided by elders and reflective thinkers in those cultures. We cannot here follow this route in as much detail as it deserves; yet we can look at some examples from the history of Western philosophy. Unfortunately, all come from within the Indo-European language family. Were we to turn to the Semitic languages Hebrew and Arabic, to Chinese, or to languages native to the Americas, Africa, or the Pacific archipelagoes, we would find a much wider range of diversity.[4] But that would take us too far afield. For our purposes, we limit ourselves to three passages: from Plato, a Greek; from Immanuel Kant, a German; and from David Hume, an English-speaking Scot.

First, we consider Plato. In Greek, nouns have five cases and three genders (masculine, feminine, and neuter). In addition, nouns inflect for number: singular, dual, and plural. Among the cases, the *nominative* is used as the subject of any verb and as the completion of "to be" or other copula; the *vocative* is used to address somebody directly; the *accusative* is the direct object of a verb and can be used to specify a part, character, or quality or to indicate extent of time or space; the *genitive* usually limits the meaning of another noun by indicating possession, the subject or object of an action or feeling, material or contents, measure or cause, although by extension these relations can apply to verbs; and the *dative* limits a verb by indicating that *to* or *for* which something is done.

Greek inflects the verb as well, to indicate variations of time and status. More important, it can modify many of the forms into infinitives (or verbal nouns) and participles (or verbal adjectives) that can themselves be inflected by case as nominative, accusative, genitive, or dative. While functioning as verbs in their own right, participles and infinitives may also play a role as constituents of the main sentence; like subordinate conjunctions in that they introduce and integrate fully-fledged clauses, they contribute a complex set of subsidiary actions to that of the main verb.[5]

As a result, by using participial, as well as standard subordinate, clauses to modify various terms, classical Greek can construct very intricate sentences. It avoids ambiguity because inflection specifies the role of each term and clause vis-à-vis the main verb.

4 Such possibilities have long been suggested for non-Indo-European languages, initially by Wilhelm von Humboldt – *Schriften zur Sprachphilosophie, Werke in fünf Bänden III*, ed. A. Flitner and K. Giel (Darmstadt: Wissenschaftliche Buchgesellschaft, 1963), and *Essays on Language*, ed. T. Harden and D. Farrelly, trans. John Wieczorek and Ian Roe (Frankfurt am Main and New York: P. Lang, 1997) – and later by Whorf – *Language, Thought and Reality*. In working towards the conclusions of this chapter, I looked at the relation between the conventions of classical Hebrew and the reasoning of the Talmudic rabbis.

5 For these comments on Greek syntax, I rely on W. Goodwin, *A Greek Grammar* (Boston: Ginn & Co., 1892).

When we turn to a passage from Plato's *Cratylus*, we find him explaining what goes on when we want to use words to characterise what is and is not.[6] Socrates proceeds by drawing analogies between speaking or naming, on the one hand, and other instrumental activities, such as cutting, burning, weaving, boring, sailing, and music-making, on the other. Like cutting and burning, speaking is constrained by the nature of the material acted on; like weaving and boring, it requires an appropriate instrument; like weaving again, it has a specific purpose and an agent using the instrument for that purpose; like weaving, boring, or blacksmithing, its appropriate instrument must be formed according to a rule; and as in weaving, boring, music-making, and shipbuilding, the instrument used and rule followed must be adjusted with reference to the specific nature of what is acted on, so that it is the skilled user who judges the success of the manufacturer's work.

Thus the effect of these various analogical inferences is to explain speaking or naming as an action that uses an instrument (a word) on some material (the reality communicated) according to a rule, so that we can describe accurately whatever is, taking account of the constraints imposed by this content, and effectively enough to satisfy a competent speaker (or dialectician), who judges whether the speaking captures what is being communicated.

The plausibility of this complex explanation is grounded in the conventions of Greek syntax. The instrumental use of the dative can specify the role words play relative to the speaker (who would be in the nominative case) and to the content spoken (accusative). The material sense of the genitive serves to distinguish the reality referred to from the actual import of the words. An infinitive ("to describe accurately") is able to articulate the purpose to be achieved. Participles, such as "applying a rule" and "considering constraints," adjust and qualify the central action. And subordinate clauses specify what rule to apply and who sets the standard. In other words, Greek syntactical conventions provide a template within which Plato elaborates a network of tendrils that show what happens when we "speak truly what is and what is not."

6 *Cratylus*, 387c–390d, trans. C.D.C. Reeve, in *Plato: Complete Works*, ed. Cooper, 106–9.

Second, we turn to Immanuel Kant. German has only four cases – nominative, genitive, dative, and accusative – indicating how nouns, adjectives, or pronouns are connected to the verb and allowing a sentence to start with a dative or accusative without confusion. As well, nouns can be masculine, feminine, or neuter in gender, so that participles and pronouns, even of inanimate objects, can be easily connected with their referent. Complex nouns are constructed by melding several components together (for example, *Reiseschreibmappe* = "travelling writing case"), removing the need for unnecessary genitives or prepositional phrases. In addition to inflected participles and infinitives, German has both a gerund, or verbal noun, and a gerundive, or verbal adjective, based on the gerund.

The placing of the components of a verb phrase follows fairly strict rules. The verb form that is inflected to match the subject is the second item in the sentence, whereas any infinitives or participles that complete the construction come at the end ("He has to the Yankees by the Blue Jays traded been"). Similarly, when a simple verb has a separable prefix, that prefix is delayed until the rest of the sentence has been said ("She sent the package with her gift for Dana off"). Within a subordinate clause, both the beginning and the end, are marked: introduced with a conjunction and then all verbs are held in abeyance until its close, with the inflected form bringing up the rear ("The man who to the store some bread to buy gone has ..."). Participles and infinitives conclude the constructions they govern, even when there is no initiating term. When participles (or verbal adjectives) modify a noun, they go between the article ("a" or "the") and its noun and follow the nouns and adverbs they govern ("The on the hill of brick built house").[7]

As a result of these rules, listeners or readers never lose their place in a complex sentence, which embeds subordinate clauses one within another, because no clause ends until its primary verb has emerged. This is why German can construct very long sentences, which have only one primary verb but a number of subordinate constructions:

---

7 On occasion, one finds something similar in English, but the phrase is tied together with hyphens: "with an I-turn-the-crank-of-the-Universe air" (Lowell), cited by Otto Jespersen, *Growth and Structure of the English Language* (Leipzig: Teubner; Oxford: Blackwell, 1926), §17, 14.

descriptions in apposition, conditions, circumstances of various sorts, purpose, results, modifiers of nouns either as participles or as clauses, and so on. The sentence (as well as each component) remains in suspense until the participles and infinitives of the central verb fall into place, making the whole thing happen.

In his *Critique of Pure Reason*, Kant sets out to explain how it is that humans know that every event has a cause. His solution integrates a number of functions. We passively become aware of things in the world through our sensible intuition, but these experiences are always formed by the temporal and spatial settings in which they occur. To understand what is given to us in these intuitions, we need to organize them according to some basic conventions that define number, reality, relations, and modalities. Traditional logic, in its table of logical judgments, provides a clue to the basic set of conventions, and cause is the principle reflected in the conditional *if-then* sentence. This particular concept or category can be regularly applied to our experience because the causal sequence has the same basic schema as the flow of experienced time. To distinguish a causal sequence from one that is simply contingent on its subjective temporal setting, however, we need some rule – and that is provided by the principle of sufficient reason. Wherever we can give a sufficient reason for things happening in the order they do, we can apply the concept of cause. Further, since we apply cause to the time and space of appearances, and cannot reach back to the way things really are, it is at least possible for some real things to act freely or in an uncaused way.

Here we have a complex of operations working together to generate the simple judgment that "every event has a cause." Just as German syntactical conventions make it possible to subordinate a number of clauses into a single, clearly articulated sentence, Kant has taken a number of operations and shown how they contribute to our understanding of causal necessity. Each operation is self-contained and can be analysed in detail. But together, they fit into a larger pattern, where each has its distinctive role to play : intuition, though passive, provides the content for understanding's judgments; we can distinguish that content from the subjective spatio-temporal form in which it appears; understanding's most fundamental judgment forms derive from those of traditional logic; it can apply those forms to intuition's content because they correspond to the latter's spatio-temporal forms; the resulting judgments apply only to things as they appear, not as they are in themselves; and further, the principle of sufficient reason constrains the act of judging.

In English, for clarity, one prefers to separate each of those operations into a separate proposition and then suggest how they relate to each other. But German prefers to link them together eloquently into one long, complex, yet carefully articulated sentence, where the act of judging serves as the integrating verb and the role of each component is clearly indicated. Much in the way a German sentence is able to integrate a large number of subordinate constructions into a single period, Kant's explanation describes the way a number of functions fit together to produce our conviction that every event has a cause. Syntax provides the framework within which he was able to explore tentacles of interconnection.

Third and finally, we look at David Hume's explanation for the same phenomenon: our belief that every event has a cause. English is largely an uninflected language, although it distinguishes plurals from singulars. The masculine, feminine, and neuter genders and inflected signs for the accusative case, however, are restricted to personal pronouns. Some nouns and relative conjunctions can form a possessive case, which resembles the Greek and German genitives but, unlike them, indicates primarily ownership or origin. Apart from distinguishing singulars from plurals, the signs for nouns remain the same wherever they appear in a sentence. Word order and uninflected particles such as prepositions and conjunctions indicate their connection to the rest of the sentence.

In general, the subject precedes the verb, while objects, both direct and indirect, follow.[8] But the location of any subordinate clause needs to be carefully considered. Clauses modifying the action of the verb can stand at the beginning, or directly after its object; those modifying nouns, as close as possible to those nouns. It is thus hard

---

8 Jespersen (ibid., §14, 10) had his "pupils calculate statistically various points in regard to word-order in different languages." He presents "the percentage ... of sentences in which the subject precedes the verb and the latter in its turn preceded its object." The results had nineteenth- and early- twentieth- century English writers ranging from 82% (Macauley) to 97% for prose and 81% to 88% for poetry. In contrast, Goethe's poetry had only 30%, and Tovote, a contemporary German prose writer, 31%. Because English personal pronouns retain distinct objective and possessive cases, they do allow some exceptions to this rule: "Thee do I love ..."

to distinguish between places where several clauses are to qualify the same primary term and places where the second clause modifies a noun or verb within the first (as in "the house by the gas station with a red roof"). So there is a strong preference for reasonably straightforward subject-verb-object sentences, with a limited number of subordinate constructions, if any. A complex thought finds expression in a series of such independent sentences, with any connection coming from some convenient adverb or adjective.[9]

English has a number of strategies for turning verbs into nouns or substantives. This makes it possible to interconnect actions in ways other than by participles and subordinate clauses. The present participle, which adds "-ing" to the verb, can serve as a noun (called a "gerund"), which can at the same time govern several objects, have a subject, and so on: "The teacher's angrily *sending* the boy to the office was wrong." In addition, there are what Jespersen calls "nexus-substantives": words such as "arrival," "belief," and "fight"[10] and nouns that one creates by adding "-ation" to a verb: "realization," "departmentalization." This strategy can produce sentences in which all the action happens in nominal constructions and the verb is just the bare copula: "is." Such actions can no longer be linked by clauses and participial constructions but require prepositions that originally served to connect nouns that name things.[11]

---

9 Indeed, English has a tendency to prefer short, often monosyllabic, words and simplified expressions. "As an Englishman does not like to use more words or syllables than are strictly necessary, so he does not like to say more than he can stand to." Ibid., §11, 7.

10 Otto Jespersen, *Analytic Syntax* (New York: Holt Rinehart & Winston, 1969), 57ff.

11 Unfortunately, this practice, frequent in academic writing, lengthens the sentence and indeed makes it more difficult to see how various actions relate to each other, since the main verb is often a simple copula. For example, consider the following sentence from John Dewey's *Reconstruction in Philosophy* (New York, Mentor: 1953), 119: "The *isolation* of *thinking* from *confrontation* with facts encourages that kind of *observation* which merely accumulates brute facts, which occupies itself laboriously with mere details, but never inquires into their meaning and consequences – a safe *occupation,* for it never contemplates any *use* to be made of the observed facts in *determining* a plan for *changing* the situation."

An English-language journalist once introduced me to the concept of a "fog index." "Fog" increases in English when one uses long words in long sentences. Dewey's greater fog, when compared with an author like Jane Austen, may result from attempting to express a Germanic type of complexity.

Hume's explanation for our claim that all events have causes adopts a quite different strategy from Kant's. Thoughts are not brought to our intuitive sensations by the understanding. Rather, the ideas that function "in thinking and reasoning" are "the faint images" of the impressions of sensations and reflections.[12] Ideas come to be associated with each other in only three ways: they resemble each other; they are next to each other in time and space; and cause and effect. Because our experiences do not provide any impression from which we could derive the idea of cause, Hume has to look elsewhere for its origin. He finds it in the fact that in our experiences some events are repeated, always coming in the same order, one after another. This constant conjunction produces in the mind a tendency or habit, so that it inevitably moves from the idea of one to the idea of the other. It is the impression of this customary habit that grounds our idea of cause. And that grounding is sufficiently strong for Hume to adopt a fully deterministic view of human action.[13]

In this explanation, things produce impressions; impressions produce ideas; and ideas produce words.[14] We have a sequence of simple actions where one thing generates something else, which becomes productive in its turn, rather like the way simple subject-verb-object sentences follow in a sequence when one wants to avoid confusing clauses. At each level, we have individual items – things, impressions, ideas, words – lacking any particular reference to anything outside themselves, apart from what they might do, rather like English nouns that retain the same form no matter what their context in the sentence, even as subjects of verbs.

Our idea of cause emerges from a more complex sequence. One impression (or idea) follows another, much as object follows subject in an English sentence. This happens not just once but several times: an impression (or idea) of one type follows an impression (or idea) of the second type again and again. They are plural instances of a single type; and they are not affected by their diverse contexts, just as an English noun can be plural, but otherwise remain identical wherever it appears. The fact that this movement from one to the other

---

12 David Hume, *A Treatise of Human Nature* (Harmondsworth: Penguin, 1969), I, I, 1, 49.

13 Ibid., II, iii, 1: "Of Liberty and Necessity," 447–55.

14 See above, chapter 2.

has recurred in the mind a number of times generates an expectation that it will happen again in the future. This expectation becomes, as it were, the verb that links subject to object.[15]

When we compare the simplicity of this explanation, derived from unchanging atomic units and sequences of causal action from subject to object, to the more complex explanatory moves of Plato and Kant, we see how it remains close to the conventions of English syntax and avoids the intricate interrelations that occur in inflected languages. That correspondence helps to explain its reception as the dominant philosophical paradigm of the Anglo-Saxon world.

In other words, Hume's explanation has a structure that resembles the way good English style thrives on simple, monosyllabic words and favours short, independent, subject-verb-object sentences that follow one another in a sequence.

So there does seem to be some correspondence between the grammatical possibilities available when speaking a language and the kinds of hypotheses that reflective thinkers in that culture propose. When looking for an explanation, we may well draw, consciously or subconsciously, on the syntax of our native language as a way of linking together a variety of components. It offers a template into which we fit the features we want to explain; and it points towards tendrils, implicit in our concepts but not yet noticed. In other words, the syntactical conventions of a language by which the central verb integrates the various components of a sentence, and by which sentences relate to each other, can influence the quest for the tendrils required to integrate explanatory proposals.

15 Establishing universal causal determinism requires a much more complex psychological process.

16

Ideas and Concepts

WE STARTED THIS PILGRIMAGE with Frege's sharp separation between ideas and concepts. Ideas are the product of the subjective
experiences of the people who have them. They trace their sense back
to some particular sensation; they have links with other ideas in an
individual's history; they absorb emotional flavour from the contexts
in which they have emerged. Concepts, in contrast, are objective and
independent of what any one person happens to think. They enable
genuine communication, for several people can be thinking the same
concept, even though those intellectual acts are in different bodies
and occur within different streams of consciousness. And they provide
essential building blocks for disciplined reasoning and reflection.

The argument of this study has been that we do not need to place
these two kinds of entities in different realms, one in the human mind
and the other in a Platonic heaven. By showing how various intellectual functions can build on each other, and by recognizing how interaction with other people in learning our language regularly exposes
our prejudices, we have suggested how thoughts can be divorced from
the particular circumstances in which they emerge. Once this happens, through careful definitions, well-justified syntheses, and a disciplined checking of concepts against reality, we develop thoughts that
are sufficiently objective and independent of our subjective interests
that they cannot be distinguished from Frege's concepts.

In the course of this itinerary, I have suggested that the sense of a
concept is not an independent atom. It embodies tendrils of meaning that reach out towards other thoughts. Some of these stem from
the act of definition itself; others are gradually built into a term in the
light of both scientific investigation and the accumulated experience

of the centuries; still others radiate out from a verb or clause, looking for compatriots that flesh out its determinate meaning, providing a framework for explanations.

In the end, however, we have discovered that, even when working within the realm of pure thoughts, we do not escape relativism. The networks of meaning that have developed to explain the world in which we live frequently reflect the particular conventions of the languages we speak. Conceptual tendrils grow out of distinctive cultural practices, frustrating our quest for universal and objective concepts. For all the impressive achievements of the natural sciences in making our concepts comprehensive, even the most successful theory is in principle fallible: new discoveries, emerging from alternate perspectives, could show it to be incomplete and partial; new conceptual explanations may reveal the hidden prejudices of our particular culture. When we turn to the realm of human affairs, it is virtually impossible to find critical tests that decisively eliminate candidates for a viable social theory. We may define concepts in detail, and integrate all their components into a single, complex sense, yet still lack what we have called "comprehensiveness"; competing ways of understanding the world not only have plausibility, but are also able to explain away discrepancies.

We cannot escape relativism by postulating a Platonic realm of eternal concepts to be discovered. That endeavour turns out to be indistinguishable from the quest for comprehensiveness I described above. The fallible nature of all our ways of understanding the world cannot be avoided and raises the virtue of humility to an ethical standard that should govern all serious reflection on the nature of reality.

There is a notable implication of this limit on our conceptual achievements. We live in a world where decisions have to be made, and the best ones are based on a solid grasp of the nature of things – the likely or merely possible effects that will follow from our actions. Since our actions will impinge directly on the world around us, we should take into account not only the general structure of things and the way that will influence what happens, but also the way these actions fit into the particular circumstances of the immediate present. Yet, under the pressure of time, we cannot undertake a long and inconclusive quest for adequate comprehension. As a result, our decisions are inevitably affected by the subjectivity and relativity that bedevils ideas, quite apart from the influence our interests and particular perspectives would have on our considerations. So we live most of our lives – and do most of our thinking – within a world in which the reflective discipline of pure concepts and the immediacy of ideas intertwine inextricably. Indeed, the mixture extends over a wide range, from the immediacy of passionate reactions to unexpected events to the calm reflection of experienced and careful managers.

There are a number of ways in which the limitations of our subjective world condition our thinking. We are emotional creatures, and our response to events depends as much on how we feel as what we think. Indeed, it is just these passions that often stimulate us to act. Because they are so immediate and vivid, we easily assume that other people react in the same way. We appeal to empathy – the sharing of feelings – both to communicate our situation and to infer what is happening with our fellows. Yet feelings and emotions are notoriously volatile; and the typology of human behavioural types developed through a number of tests (such as the Myers-Briggs) has shown that people react in quite diverse ways to the world around them. Emotions do not provide a solid basis for communication or for reaching a shared understanding; yet they are intrinsic to much of our mental functioning. Their subjective focus frustrates disciplined reflection.

It is not only feelings that condition our thinking. We also interpret much of our world in the light of the particular experiences through which we have lived. We are not immediately aware of our limitations; and we regularly take what happens to us in our space and time as normative for all – as what would happen anywhere and in any context. And so our ideas – as generalizations from our experience – seem authoritative and comprehensive. When events happen, each person notices and focuses on those immediate elements and features that are most critical to them. When a number of observers generalize from these perceptions and interactions, they do not all do so in the same way; as a result of their various developmental histories, they emphasise and ignore different features and aspects. For all that we might assume that we are talking about the same thing, then, we often draw on diverse associations and interconnections.

In the previous chapter, I suggested that even the languages we speak shape our conceptual explanations. Rather than reaching a way of integrating components into a single thought that is plausible for any thinking person, we draw on peculiarities of our culture and assume that they not only are shared by other cultures, but also capture the way the world is. The conditioning influence of our particular setting in time, place, and society relativizes our efforts to communicate with each other and to understand reality.

The fact that we are seldom aware of our limitations has a significant impact. To act with decisiveness, we need to believe that we are moving in the proper way, and this implies that, for the moment at least, we are certain of what we are doing and why. Familiar with the world of our experience, and lacking challenges to our worldview, we assume that it holds for all people and for all time. We can dismiss whatever opposition emerges by attributing it to evil motives or to the distorting influence of circumstances. We easily notice the speck of subjectivity in the eye of our opponent, while remaining blissfully ignorant of the huge blob of subjectivity that has found a place in our own.

Support for this conviction of rectitude is frequently derived from some authority that (or who) has escaped from the fallibility of our world (we assume) and speaks with an unequivocal voice. Abandoning the humility of disciplined conceptual thought (if we ever subscribed to it), we adopt some version of infallibility and move forward with confidence not only in our interactions with compatriots in the social and political arena, but also in the way we treat our natural environment. In all these ways, the ideas that we have acquired over the course of our lives, and which inevitably retain a relative and subjective focus, mould our life in the world.

It would seem, then, that the quest for comprehensive objectivity that marks the disciplined development of conceptual thought is doomed to failure. The partiality of our experience as individuals condemns us to living in a world of conflicting opinions, where "truth" is a suspect term, since it betrays an assumption of infallibility.

However, for all that our intellectual life seldom escapes the relativism and subjectivity of ideas, it is equally full of conceptual content. We may find it difficult to achieve full, objective comprehensiveness, but we none the less regularly communicate with each other; we are able in some measure to move outside of our limited frameworks and understand what others are saying. Few of us may have the ease with which pure mathematicians manipulate concepts, but at the same time few of us are completely inarticulate.

For, just as the relativism of subjectivity can range from the individualism of pure egotism to sharing the preconceptions of our group, culture, or historical era (usually the present), so also conceptual objectivity can manifest diverse degrees of comprehensiveness.

We start by using language to communicate with family and neighbours. Through trial and error, we discover the words that tell other people what we originally had in mind, and we modify our understanding of terms until we respond appropriately to our parents and friends. Gradually, we develop a sense of common and shared meanings that extend beyond our immediate circle and incorporate the world of strangers, both near and far. In addition, we develop a sense of how to integrate words into complex sentences.

As this skill develops, we learn to ask for and develop definitions. Rather than simply absorbing common senses from trial and error, we reflect on the world of shared meanings and turn to dictionaries that tell us the prevailing standards of our culture. Whenever we confront disagreement and conflict, we develop the ability to articulate the specific sense we have in mind and compare it with that of our opponent so that we can come to a common understanding.

We find that such thoughts incorporate tendrils that implicate other meanings. These are not simply the residue of past experiences – associations that recur in the stream of our consciousness. Initially, they are implicit in our definitions, but their range expands as we discover regular patterns in the world that are independent of our particular expectations and experiences. These tendrils link with others that reach out from related thoughts, enabling us to construct intricate syntheses and complex unities. Because they depend on shared and publicly defined meanings, they are not personal and subjective associations, but are rather grounded in the interpersonal world of words and thoughts. The thought of "some" leads to the thought of "others" not just for us, but for anyone who understands the limits inherent in the original concept.

It is not simply the interaction with other intelligent beings with whom we communicate that moves us to refine our thoughts. We also live in the world. Many of our thoughts start from our efforts to make sense of the environment so that we can anticipate what will happen. Such generalizations are constantly subject to correction, as we find that expectations do not materialize and the world does not fit our preconceptions. Learning from our failures, and becoming more confident in the light of our specific successes, we refine our thoughts so that they take account of the way the world really is. We find that some explanatory frameworks are more objective and comprehensive than others – less likely to be confounded by inconvenient facts. The results of controlled experiment and disciplined observation shape the interpersonal world of communication and discourse, refining the meanings of terms, adjusting the syntax of our language, and creating a cultural realm that not only extends beyond our immediate society and age, but stretches back through generations and opens up a future of investigation and ongoing elaboration.

Permeating this whole development is our native ability to become aware of our partiality. We discover how other people are different. Rather than simply assuming that they are wrong, we learn why they say and do what they do. We allow our thoughts to be put in question and seek some conceptual framework that will do justice not only to what is valid in our original views, but also to the natural and social world around us. Through these encounters, we learn humility and come to realize that, however strong the grounds of our present convictions, they are inevitably fallible. It may always be possible to find a more comprehensive conceptual picture that does full justice not only to our experience, but also to the disciplined experience of others, and which bridges the differences in a more comprehensive way.

In the previous chapter, for example, I not only showed that our native languages may lead us to think in quite different ways; I did so using English to indicate and characterize the differences. For all of its limitations, I used it to illustrate the way other languages organize sentences and thoughts and opened up a more universal context in which speakers of different languages can interact and learn from one another. The tendrils in our syntax are not chains binding us to partial perspectives, but can be adopted and adapted to create a more open, tolerant, and inclusive understanding of the fabric of our global society.

If, on the one hand, our ideas – whether immediate reactions or developed prejudices – inevitably affect our active life in the world, on the other hand, as reflective thinkers, we are able to overcome subjectivity and relative perspectives and grasp the principles that objectively govern the way the world. Our intellectual life is as much one as it is the other. When we are thinking, we may on occasion be simply associating ideas from our stream of consciousness, but we may also be tracing the tendrils that link concept to concept. Both moves are psychological, but one is in danger of removing us from our fellows and our world, while the other explores principles of the universe that have emerged over the centuries of our human existence and have become part of our common thoughts.

What is misleading in Frege's analysis, then, is not its sharp distinction between the relativism of ideas and the universality of concepts. It is that the distinction becomes a barrier that requires quite different intellectual operations on its two sides. What I have presented in this story as an alternative is the picture of a continuum that stretches from inarticulate immersion in personal experience to the reflective articulation of thoughts that capture and structure the accumulated experience of generations – an accumulation preserved in written texts and (less effectively) in the artefacts left behind for archaeologists to decipher. It is not that some people are limited to their own consciousness while others function almost as disembodied minds. Rather, all of us range up and down the spectrum, at times reacting unthinkingly to perceived insults, at times reflectively considering all sides of a question and working with others to find effective solutions to the demands of both the natural and the social worlds. The human intellect integrates the diversity of personal experience and behavioural type with the realm of common and shared concepts that enable us to anticipate the future with some measure of accuracy. "Ideas" and "concepts" name the two extremes of this dynamic field, extremes that interact reciprocally to maintain a constant tension. They define the life of mind.

Epilogue

THE LIFE OF MIND IS A DYNAMIC FIELD OF FORCES that intersect with and affect each other. We have been looking at a part of this rich complex – the tension between what Frege called "ideas" and "concepts." Since our thinking always takes place within our bodies – in a specific place and at a specific time – its stimulus inevitably comes from individual and particular interests and experiences. Yet we have seen how the mind transforms such subjective content, through the operation of a number of functions, into something more objective and universal. Our thinking can aspire towards a fully comprehensive understanding of the way the world is. Demanding passions and the need for immediate and decisive action challenge the dispassionate reflection that looks for adequate concepts. At the same time, the failure to achieve our ends when we respond simply to subjective interests pushes us to investigate and discover ways of thinking about the world that more adequately predict what will happen when we act. The spirited interplay between ideas and concepts dominates our intellectual life.

For all of the interrelationship between these two poles, however, we must not confuse them. Concepts, in sharp contrast to ideas, have deliberately recognized the subjectivity and relativity of our immediate thoughts and looked for a sense that is more universal – that does justice to what is important in the subjective variety by identifying what is common. Conceptual objectivity manifests a range in breadth, starting with the early ability to communicate with our families, extending through our cultural education and encounters with other languages and people, to our checks against experience to determine which thoughts effectively capture the nature of reality.

What is distinctive about concepts is that they are the tools of communication. As Frege says, no two people have the same idea of a horse; none the less they have a common understanding that enables them to distinguish horses from other animals and, working together, to train them for racing, ploughing, dressage, or war. Concepts have facilitated the development of a whole industry for breeding horses. And those thoughts are not specific to a single groom or trainer, but retain their sense when transferred to others and adopted by later generations.

To be sure, that sense is not fixed in a Platonic heaven. It adapts in the light of experience, of trial and error, of encounters with other horse-breeding cultures. Concepts are not static, but dynamic; some aspects atrophy and disappear over time; others surface as novelties; and each kind of change alters the significance of the central term. The interpersonal dynamic of communication allows this flexibility and enrichment as new features noticed by some individuals gain acceptance in the larger community. While subcultures may develop distinctive vocabularies, it always remains possible for diverse groups to interact and develop a common and inclusive language.

While ideas are located specifically in the individual who entertains them, concepts abide in a quite different realm. To be sure, they are thought by singular men and women, but they are independent of any particular instantiation. They carry their meanings across cultures and continue as generations pass away. The discovery of writing has facilitated this transmission, but oral cultures as well remember the teaching of the elders and retain, almost verbatim, their spoken traditions. There is, then, what we might call a "conceptual realm," with its ground in the lives of individual thinking beings across the ages, but which none the less has a life of its own that continues to function as the individuals who do the thinking are born, grow to maturity, and die.

The dynamic of this conceptual realm deserves some consideration. It is not simply a function of the material substratum within which it exists. To be sure, the content of our thoughts emerges out of experience. But that content is refined and altered through a number of distinct processes, which become progressively more reflective and deliberate. Each one liberates our thoughts from the immediacy of our own sensations and bodily reactions.

Initially, there is the encounter with other people. As we learn to articulate our thoughts in words, we adopt the vocabulary of those around us. In doing so, we learn, through trial and error, to refine the sense of each term so that others will understand what we want to tell them, and we will do what others ask us to do. This involves an implicit kind of reflection. No longer do we respond immediately to our experiences, but we stop and think about them. The words we use and the specific senses we communicate are formed by the conscious awareness of how our perspectives frequently diverge from those of our neighbours and by the effort to reach an agreed understanding.

Self-conscious reflection is largely implicit in our early use of language. But it can become explicit as well. In the story we derived from Hegel's psychology, he shows how thoughts find expression in a shared language. Then he makes a peculiar move. He talks about memory not primarily as the effort to recall something that has happened, but as the habitual association of word and sense. This can develop into what is called "mechanical memory": the ability to use words without thinking about their meaning, whether the recitation of an overly familiar prayer or poem or a rambling discourse that draws on the formulae of our daily conversation. By developing this skill, the mind frees itself from its feelings and associations to focus dispassionately on the words themselves. It considers these words as thoughts that are independent of personal interests and perspectives. It is this ability to reflect on pure thoughts that triggers the move to what we have called "concepts." Once we begin to think about our thoughts as such, we can define them by distinguishing carefully one from another, we can clarify the way they link together and integrate into more complex concepts, and we can formulate what kind of "effects that might conceivably have practical bearings, we conceive the object of our conception to have."[1] These anticipations of practical consequences then become the basis for testing how comprehensive our concepts actually are.

The course of this reflection becomes clear in terms of the comparisons and differentiations, the implications and tendrils, that emerge from the act of reflective thinking. While these operations may correlate to particular constellations of neurons in some brain or other, those physiological events cannot explain the inferences, which rather reflect the moves initiated by thought itself. Concepts and their interconnections can be communicated and shared with

1 Peirce, "How to Make Our Ideas Clear," 5.402.

other people who have their own distinctive brains; they can jump from neural system to neural system without significant alteration. Reasoning works as effectively in one mind as it does in the next.

Thus what we have is a realm of existence that functions on its own terms, in ways that are quite independent of the material substratum within which it occurs. If there is any causal movement between body and mind, it would seem to emerge from the latter, for auditors start to think about the definitions and explanations they hear not because of the particular sounds that have reached their ears and the signals transmitted to their brain, but because of the sense associated with those sounds, which is in no way identical with them. (We do, after all, easily differentiate homonyms.) Whatever neurological effects emerge in the brain are a result of that thinking, not the other way around.

The conceptual realm then is clearly distinct from the material or physical realm explored by the natural sciences. Rather than the stimulus–response pattern of cause and effect, which tends to move along a linear and sequential path, it works with reasons, in which the results of drawing implications can influence the originating concept, and the end in view can be as effective in triggering an inference as any initiating impetus. One can understand its development and explain the way it adapts and changes without recourse to the physiology of the thinkers or the physics of their brain cells.

To be sure, many of these changes may be reactions to lived experience. But events have their impact on the realm of meaning because the mind grasps them in conceptual terms; what happens is either anticipated or a surprise. On their own, events are simply physical phenomena. At the same time, concepts are not only integrated and related to each other in the process of deliberation, but can also result in physical action, changing the course of nature. While the physical and the conceptual realms continuously interact, that does not mean that they operate according to the same kind of laws and conditions. They simply intersect in the bodies of thinking individuals, where an event has both a neurological and a conceptual dimension. What triggers that event can sometimes be traced back to sensations and bodily chemistry, sometimes to a network of thoughts; and its effects can be equally diverse.[2] It is, however, only the network of

---

2 Note that this "dualism" is between the physical and the conceptual, not between the physical and consciousness, for the latter is as much the subject of immediate experience, conditioned as it is by our bodies, as of thought.

thoughts that transcends the limits of the particular body and develops a life with its own internal dynamic, one that is not only interpersonal, but also international and intergenerational.

In this realm of concepts, the initiative comes then not from external causes, but from the deliberation of reflective thinking. Even at the most basic level of linguistic communication, we notice the extent to which individuals use words in different ways, as well as how much we agree. This reflection then enables us to define more adequate general concepts that do justice to both aspects. We construct complex concepts by working out with care how the various terms fit together. We learn from experience when we are aware not only of the way our thoughts anticipate future effects in the world, but also of how those events confirm or disappoint our expectations. This whole process is not just the surface play of physical and biological causes. Each move is justified by the sense of the terms being thought, the way they interconnect, and the way experience confirms conceptual predictions. Here, there is no simple sequence of stimulus and response. Thought intercedes and mediates, weighing meanings and linking senses. And this process happens not simply within the thinking of a single individual, but in the deliberations of councils and task forces, of teams of researchers and panels of judges, of the community of intelligent agents. This deliberative and reflective feature is the defining feature of the conceptual realm.

Mathematics is the discipline that works, almost exclusively, with concepts. Theoretical physics looks for mathematical formulae that capture essential features of the natural world. Several illustrations from these disciplines can reinforce the argument I have been putting forth. The role of mathematics, which now recognizes that there is no necessary relation between its theorems and the real world, is described by Donal O'Shea in *The Poincaré Conjecture*:[3]

The objects of mathematics lie outside common experience, however. If one doesn't define these objects carefully, one cannot manipulate them meaningfully or talk to others about them.

Artists and humanists embrace complexity and ambiguity. Mathematicians, in contrast, work by obsessively defining terms and stripping off extraneous

---

3 Donal O'Shea, *The Poincaré Conjecture* (New York: Walker & Co., 2007), 46–7.

meaning. The almost neurotic insistence that every term be rigorously defined, and every statement proved, ultimately frees one to imagine and talk about the unimaginable. Most people, traumatized by school experiences of mathematics, know all too well that mathematics is the most meticulous and demanding of disciplines, but few get to see that it is also the most liberating and imaginative of all human activities. Absolute precision buys the freedom to dream meaningfully.[4]

But absolute precision comes at a price. Terms need very careful definitions, and every statement, even the seemingly obvious, requires proof. What seems obvious can be frighteningly difficult to prove – sometimes, it even turns out to be wrong. Seemingly tiny exceptions matter, details can overwhelm, and progress can be unbearably slow. Mathematics is the only field of human endeavour where it is possible to know something with absolute certainty, but the hard work of slogging through morasses of possible definitions and formulations too often forecloses the dreamy vistas it affords to all but the few.

Having precise definitions buys the freedom to imagine. The significance of the former becomes clear in an incident that O'Shea describes. The Danish mathematician Poul Heegaard had shown "that a theorem, now known as Poincaré's duality, could not be true as stated. It turned out, [however,] that Poincaré's definition differed from Heegaard's, and the difference was crucial in allowing Poincaré's duality to work."[5] Definitions carry within them tendrils that enable some implications but not others; the specific form they take influences the inferences that reflective thought can draw from them.

Albert Einstein also stresses the freedom that comes from the use of concepts. Challenging the epistemology of Ernst Mach, whose positivism claims that scientific explanations are derived directly from the facts of experience, he notes

that even scholars of audacious spirit and fine instinct can be obstructed in the interpretation of facts by philosophical prejudices. The prejudice – which has by no means died out in the meantime – consists in the faith that

---

4 In a talk at my university, the poet Elizabeth Sewell commented that the only academics who are genuinely creative are the mathematicians. Others, she said, are primarily preserving the past.

5 O'Shea, *The Poincaré Conjecture*, 133.

facts by themselves can and should yield scientific knowledge without free conceptual construction. Such a misconception is possible only because one does not easily become aware of the free choice of such concepts, which, through verification and long usage, appear to be immediately connected with the empirical material.[6]

Earlier in the same text, Einstein articulates his epistemological credo:

I see on the one side the totality of sense-experiences, and on the other, the totality of concepts and propositions which are laid down in books. The relations between the concepts and propositions among themselves and each other are of a logical nature, and the business of logical thinking is strictly limited to the achievement of the connection between concepts and propositions among each other according to firmly laid down rules, which are the concern of logic. The concepts and propositions get 'meaning,' viz., 'content,' only through their connection with sense-experiences. The connection of the latter with the former is purely intuitive, not itself of a logical nature. The degree of certainty with which this connection, viz., intuitive combination, can be undertaken, and nothing else, differentiates empty phantasy from scientific 'truth.' The system of concepts is a creation of man together with the rules of syntax, which constitute the structure of conceptual systems. Although the conceptual systems are logically entirely arbitrary, they are bound by the aim to permit the most nearly possible certain (intuitive) and complete co-ordination with the totality of sense-experiences; secondly they aim at greatest possible sparsity of their logically independent elements (basic concepts and axioms), i.e., undefined concepts and underived [postulated] propositions.

A proposition is correct if, within a logical system, it is deduced according to the accepted logical rules. A system has truth-content according to the certainty and completeness of its co-ordination-possibility to the totality of experience. A correct proposition borrows its 'truth' from the truth-content of the system to which it belongs.[7]

6 Albert Einstein, "Autobiographical Notes," in P.A. Schlipp, ed., *Albert Einstein: Philosopher-Scientist* (New York: Tudor, 1951), 49, trans. Schlipp.

7 Ibid., 11–13. Cf. 7: "What, precisely, is 'thinking'? When, at the reception of sense-impressions, memory pictures emerge, this is not yet 'thinking.' And when such pictures form series, each member of which calls forth another, this too is not yet 'thinking.' When, however, a certain picture turns up in many series, then – precisely

Einstein implies that the freedom with which he was able to think outside the box of Newtonian space and time came from the way concepts liberated his thinking from reliance on visible experience and its appearances. At the same time, the new conceptual patterns he proposed were not arbitrary. They were responding not only to intellectual puzzles that emerged from Maxwell's theory of fields, but also to anomalies in scientific evidence that did not fit prevailing conceptions. A thorough knowledge of the results of experimental physics not only influenced the generation of his proposal of general relativity, but also suggested what kinds of experimental testing could decide between it and traditional theories. A genuinely revolutionary freedom comes not just from the ability of mathematicians to define precisely, but also from comprehensiveness – from taking seriously the "totality of experience."

Mathematics and theoretical physics provide a limiting case of the way concepts develop a life of their own that can continually interact with the immediate world of experience and scientific investigation. They refine their thoughts to exclude every possible residue of subjectivity and relativism. As such, they enable us to see in a pure form the dynamic implicit in the realm of concepts as well as its potential. The same dynamic permeates the thinking of other sciences, both natural and social, and the deliberations present everywhere in human affairs. There, one is constantly struggling, to a greater or lesser extent, to free one's thoughts from the partiality of ideas. Yet, through effective communication and careful reflection, explanations develop and prove to be both defective and effective. The same interplay between the freedom of thinking and the constraint of actual experience enables humans to understand and interact appropriately with their world. The conceptual realm has a life of its own; but finds its truth in its ability to explain effectively the world of experience.

---

through such return – it becomes an ordering element for such series, in that it connects series which in themselves are unconnected. Such an element becomes an instrument, a concept. I think that the transition from free association or 'dreaming' to thinking is characterized by the more or less dominating rôle which the 'concept' plays in it. It is by no means necessary that a concept must be connected with a sensibly cognizable and reproducible sign (word); but when this is the case thinking becomes by means of that fact communicable." I propose, I think, a more satisfactory explanation for the move from sense impressions to concepts; Einstein is perhaps still too enamoured of Hume's philosophy.

This, however, has implications for the nature of that world. We can see this in a remark of Einstein's in his dispute with quantum theory:

What does not satisfy me in that theory, from the standpoint of principle, is its attitude towards that which appears to me to be the programmatic aim of all physics: the complete description of any (individual) real situation (as it supposedly exists irrespective of any observation or substantiation).[8]

He uses this claim to set the stage for his dissatisfaction with a theory which claims that the world is not fully determinate and where critical events happen only within a range of probability. In his reaction, there is an important implication. He is suggesting that one can in principle achieve, through concepts, a "complete description of the real." By "description," he does not mean a full enumeration of specific events, but indicates, more important, a conceptual system that captures how these events are linked and related to each other. Systematic interconnection based on precise definition and the interaction of tendrils is not simply the work of our minds, but also captures what is essential about reality.

In other words, the universe is not simply a collocation of events but has an integrity that embodies links and interconnections analogous to, indeed on occasion isomorphic with, the interconnections we generate in the realm of concepts. There is an ultimate rationality inherent in the world.

For Einstein, the existence of contingencies that require descriptions using statistical probabilities rather than universal necessities calls this conviction into question. None the less even quantum theorists are making claims about the nature of reality and formulating those claims in complex conceptual terms. It could be, *pace* Einstein, that the emergence of contingency is not only a feature of the world, but also characteristic of a fully rational reflection.[9] In any case, Werner Heisenberg and Niels Bohr also claim an objective validity for their explanations and as a result implicitly suggest that the universe has a network of relations that can be captured best in theoretical terms. Science is the quest to discover explanations that describe

8 Albert Einstein, "Reply to Criticisms," in ibid., 667.
9 See my *Hegel's Systematic Contingency*.

the way the world really is – the distinctive features of its components and the links and connections that bind them together. If the best explanations turn out to be the most internally coherent, then the world itself would seem to be internally coherent as well.

If this implication has any merit, then the conceptual realm is not merely the product of human reflection over the ages, but has the potential of discerning what is essential about the universe as a whole. This means that the universe itself is integrated by means of an intricate network of tendrils that link universal patterns as well as individual facts. As Einstein says, we move from correctness to truth when our conceptual systems capture the integrated nature of our world.

So we come to the conclusion of our investigation. I have suggested that the conceptual is an immaterial realm, which has its ground in, and emerges from, the material but is not reducible to it. It has a life of its own, with its own constraints and its own kind of conditions and links. And I have suggested that the universe itself may, in its essence, have a rational structure that is amenable to comprehension through conceptual thought. One could say that we have identified a *spiritual* realm, the *divine* essence, and how humans, through their conceiving, could be the *image of god*. The only problem lies in the fact that these latter terms are not concepts but rather ideas, inevitably the product of subjective perspectives. As a result, they are understood in terms of the experience and interest of the auditor. So a claim such as that opens me either to the accusation of trying to convert the reader to some particular religion or to the charge of denying religion altogether because I am dispensing with the specific emphases of this faith or that. Discretion suggests that I abandon this final attempt at definition and limit myself instead to the language of concepts and how they relate to ideas on the one hand and to the world in itself on the other.

Acknowledgments

THIS BOOK HAS BEEN PUBLISHED through the help of a grant from the Canadian Federation for the Humanities and Social Sciences, through the Awards to Scholarly Publications Program, using funds provided by the Social Sciences and Humanities Research Council of Canada.

Because of their contributions to the development of this project, I would like to express my thanks:

- to Trent University, whose generous sabbatical policy provided me with an administrative leave in 1982–83 and a sabbatical in the winter of 1987
- to the Oxford Centre for Post-graduate Hebrew Studies (as it then was) and its president, David Patterson, for appointing me a visiting scholar for 1982–83, allowing me to explore the relation between the syntax of classical Hebrew and rabbinical reasoning in the Mishna and Talmud
- to the Social Sciences and Humanities Research Council of Canada for a release-time stipend, which facilitated an extra four months in Oxford in the autumn of 1983
- to the Department of Philosophy of Exeter University and its chair, Professor Ronald Atkinson, for making me welcome in the winter of 1987, even though its death sentence had already been pronounced
- to four anonymous readers whose vigorous criticisms exposed the fatal flaws in two previous attempts to organize my thoughts
- to Emil Fackenheim, who taught me that great philosophers are striving to escape significant dilemmas, not spinning arbitrary systems in a vacuum

- to Georg Wilhelm Friedrich Hegel. In struggling to make sense of his dense and telegraphic prose, I have constantly come upon subtle and profound insights that would never have been discovered had I explored philosophical puzzles on my own.
- to Wilfred Cantwell Smith, who encouraged my interest in languages and whom I never convinced, even after many conversations, that one has to consider concepts and their network of tendrils as well as faith and tradition when studying religion
- to Klaus Hedwig, who on several occasions converted my paratactic English into elegant, hypotactic German
- to George di Giovanni, who stubbornly resisted all my earlier attempts to escape from the fallacy of psychologism
- to Jonathan Glover, for pointing me to an important passage from William James
- to the two reviewers of this manuscript, who identified critical weaknesses in an earlier draft
- to Mark Abley, editor with McGill-Queen's University Press, for his warm encouragement and for his wise counsel on linguistic matters
- to Jacob Quinlan. Our weekly conversations have clarified many themes in this study.
- to Barbara

Index

abstraction, 16, 21, 24–5, 28, 49–52
actions, 32, 87–9, 148–50
analogy, 124–35
analysis, 60–1, 63–73, 83, 88, 137–8
argument forms, 98; argument
    from analogy, 124–35
Aristotle, 4, 66, 107–12, 116–17,
    130n9
attention, 32, 55, 58–60, 63

Bacon, Francis, 124
Bateson, Gregory, 68n4
Benveniste, Émile, 130n9, 131n10
Berkeley, George, 22, 24
British empiricists, 4–5, 20–30, 37,
    43, 49

causes, 45, 142–3, 145–6
clarity, 59–60, 64–73, 83, 87
communication, 40–3, 151, 155–6;
    of ideas, 21–4, 37–47, 50. See also
    language
comprehensiveness, 62–3, 81–91,
    99–100, 148, 151–2; of argument
    forms, 109–12, 117–22, 132–4
concepts, 91–6, 128–31, 142–3,
    147–54, 154–63; as Begriff, 4–5,

13; conceiving, 9, 15–17; objec-
    tive, 8, 15, 91–6, 154, 162–3;
    opposed to ideas, 8–9, 15, 18–19
conceptual realm, 155–63
conditional inference, 113–23
conditions, 78–9, 120–2

definition, 64–73, 100–1, 108–9,
    122–3, 151, 159
Descartes, René, 20, 58–63
differentiation, 43–5, 52–3, 59–60,
    64–73
di Giovanni, George, 6n8
dilemmas, 113–15
disjunctive syllogism, 113–23

Einstein, Albert, 159–63
emotions, 149
English language, 69–70, 143–6
exhaustive enumeration, 115
experience, 83–4
experimentation, 119
explanation, 78–9, 128, 138–46

fallibilism, 92–5, 148–50, 152
fantasy, 35
feelings, 149

finite, 100–4
Frege, Gottlob, 4–5, 13–19, 91–6, 124–5, 147, 153

Galton, Francis, 48–9
generalizing, 24, 26–30, 33, 67–8, 77–8, 149; genus, 66, 70–1, 109; words as general, 36, 43
German language, 141–3
Greek language, 139–40

Hegel, G.W.F., 5–8, 31–40, 51–2, 99–106
Humboldt, Wilhelm von, 139n4
Hume, David, 24–7, 31–3, 43, 145–6
Husserl, Edmund, 4, 13n1

ideas, 4–5, 13–14, 20–30, 32–3, 49–56, 81; and concepts, 8–9, 15, 18–19. 147–54; subjective and arbitrary, 8, 13–14, 29–30
imagination, 33–6, 58, 61, 74–5; ideas as retained images, 6, 13–14, 24–6, 48–50
induction, 109–11
inferences, 107–12, 113–23
infinite, 102–4
intuition, 32, 83–4

James, William, 48–9
Jespersen, Otto, 141n7, 143n8, 144n9

Kant, Immanuel, 23, 45–6, 75–6, 99, 128, 142–3

language, 35–6, 37–47, 50, 53–4, 136–46, 155–6. *See also* communication; syntax

Locke, John, 20–4, 37
logic, 3–4, 7–8; Hegel's *Logic*, 5–8, 99–106

mathematics, 84–5, 93, 158–61
meaning, 49–54, 79
memory, 52–8, 60, 79, 156
Mencius, 128
mental functions, 30, 36–7, 58–9
Mill, John Stuart, 4, 27–8, 109–11, 119, 121
modus ponens. See conditional inference

natural law, 118–23
necessary connection, 115, 118–19, 121–2
negation, 68
nouns: syntax of nouns, 131–2, 139, 141, 143–4

objectivity, 8–9, 55–7, 88–9, 91–6, 147–53, 154–6. *See also* comprehensiveness
O'Shea, Donal, 158–9

Paivio, Allan, 48n1
Peirce, C.S., 83
physics, 159–61
Plato, 127, 140
positive reinforcement. *See* resemblance
predictions, 82–7, 122–3, 133–4, 151–2
psychology: conceiving as psychological, 15–19, 90–2, 94; fallacy of psychologism, 4–7, 13–19, 94; laws of association, 13–14, 18, 27, 33–4, 37

real world, 21–2, 62–3, 81–9,
  109–12, 129, 151–2, 162–3
reasoning, 25–7, 55
reciprocal interaction, 40–1, 45–6,
  79, 88–9, 103–4
recognition, 39–43, 68–9
recollection, 32–3, 37, 52, 58
reflection, 95–6, 156
relativism, 148–9. *See also* subjectivity
representation, 32–3. *See also* ideas
resemblance, 26–30, 34, 43–5, 61

sensation, 21–4, 31–2
significance, 49, 54–6
signs, 35–6, 41, 44, 46–7, 77–8,
  137–8; signs and memory, 50–2,
  54–6
similarity. *See* resemblance
Stoics: on natural law, 117–18
subconscious, 32–3, 62
subjectivity, 8–9, 42–3, 54–5, 76–7,
  82, 147–53
sufficient reason, 77–8, 142
syllogisms, 107–12, 126
syntax, 129–32, 136–46

synthesis, 33–6, 61–3, 74–80,
  103–4, 137–8; resulting in unity,
  6, 75–9, 105–6

tendrils, 10, 70–3, 86–9, 147–8;
  as conditions, 78–9, 122–3; in
  inference, 99–106, 110–12,
  114–23, 129–34; as objective,
  72, 95–6, 151; and syntax, 131–2,
  136–9, 146
thoughts, 51, 57–63, 64–73, 81–9,
  158–9; between ideas and
  concepts, 5, 95, 147

understanding: in Kant, 76, 78
unity, 45–7, 76–8, resulting from
  synthesis, 6, 75–9, 105–6
universals, 108–12. *See also*
  generalizing

verbs, 125–35, 139, 141–4

Whorf, Benjamin, 131n11, 139n4
words, 21–2, 46–7, 52–6, 69–70. *See
  also* signs